DEMISE OF THE DOLLAR

DEMISE OF THE DOLLAR

FROM THE BAILOUTS TO THE PANDEMIC AND BEYOND

Third Edition

ADDISON WIGGIN

WILEY

Published by John Wiley & Sons, Inc., Hoboken, New Jersey.
Published simultaneously in Canada.

For general information on our other products and services or for technical support, please contact our Customer Care Department within the United States at (800) 762-2974, outside the United States at (317) 572-3993 or fax (317) 572-4002.

Wiley also publishes its books in a variety of electronic formats. Some content that appears in print may not be available in electronic formats. For more information about Wiley products, visit our web site at www.wiley.com.

Library of Congress Cataloging-in-Publication Data is Available:

ISBN 9781394174652 (Cloth)
ISBN 9781394175451 (ePDF)
ISBN 9781394175444 (epub)

Cover Design: Mark O'Dell
Cover Image: © Nik Merkulov/Shutterstock
SKY10044340_031023

For Jennifer, Henry, August, Elizabeth
— and Winston

"The empire will end, all empires do. And since it was financed by debt rather than by tribute, it will end in a financial disaster. The cost, I mean the money lost on the imperial adventure, will have to be reckoned with. And the only way to do that is by incinerating it in inflation."

—Bill Bonner

CONTENTS

Foreword   *xi*

Acknowledgments   *xv*

INTRODUCTION: Fistful of Dollars   1

CHAPTER 1: The Greenback Boogie   7

CHAPTER 2: "We Are All Keynesians Now"   19

CHAPTER 3: Attention to Deficits Disorder   31

CHAPTER 4: Here Comes the Boom   59

CHAPTER 5: Oops, Here's the Bust   83

CHAPTER 6: A Modern Enigma   99

CHAPTER 7: Short, Unhappy Episodes In Monetary History   111

CHAPTER 8: Alas, the Demise of the Dollar   135

Notes   *179*
Index   *189*

FOREWORD

Making monetary economics complex and inaccessible to all but experts is easy. All you have to do is follow the crowd of mainstream Ph.D. economists, use lots of jargon (like Non-Accelerating Inflation Rate of Unemployment, NAIRU, and Downward Nominal Wage Rigidity, DNWR), adopt some handy models such as the Phillips curve, and you're all set. No one will understand what you're saying, but you'll win applause from pundits and Wall Street cheerleaders who will welcome you to the club of incomprehensible insiders.

Making monetary economics straightforward and accessible to everyday Americans is hard. First you have to understand the technical concepts yourself (including their many flaws). Then you have to translate the jargon into plain English. Finally you have to write in a clear style with a strong dose of history for context and a pinch of humor.

The irony is that the accessible version is closer to the truth of how money works than the complex version.

There are two reasons for this. The first is that the jargon is . . . just jargon. I've done economic analysis at the highest levels of difficulty for more than 40 years, and I've yet to encounter a concept that could not be clearly stated in plain English. For example, downward nominal wage rigidity just means that people don't like pay cuts. Non-accelerating inflation rate of employment means that if labor is scarce, wages and inflation go up as a result. Is it really so difficult to write plainly? The answer: it's not difficult at all if you're willing to shed the suit of armor jargon most economists wear to bed.

The second reason is that most of the models used by economists (and the jargon used to describe them) are simply wrong. I once examined the list of all winners of the Nobel Prize in Economics and discovered that about one-third of the prizes were given for contributions that are completely false.

Ben Bernanke won the prize in 2022 for research on banks and financial crises, yet his leadership at the Federal Reserve caused the worst financial crisis since the Great Depression and led to the failures of Bear Stearns, Fannie Mae, Freddie Mac, and Lehman Brothers. Eugene Fama won in 2013 for his theory of efficient markets, but markets are not efficient at all; they're wild and unpredictable and subject to crashes and bubbles. To be clear, there are some notable winners who made solid contributions to economics, but many of the prizes were given for junk science.

The biggest joke of all is that the Nobel Prize in Economics is not even a real Nobel Prize. The original Nobel Prizes were awarded for Physics, Chemistry, Medicine, Literature, and Peace beginning in 1901. In 1969, the Swedish Central Bank created the Sveriges Riksbank Prize in Economic Sciences in Memory of Alfred Nobel funded by the central bank; the original Nobel Prizes were funded by the estate of Alfred Nobel. You can think of the Nobel Prize in Economics as a wannabe prize frequently awarded for ideas that don't hold water.

Another example of junk science in economics is the Phillips curve. This is not just some arcane theory; it's at the center of Federal Reserve interest rate policy today. The theory is that low unemployment causes higher inflation, and high unemployment reduces inflation. The relationship between unemployment and inflation can be represented on a graph as a downward-sloping curve. The only problem with the theory is that it's not true. The period in the late 1960s did see low unemployment and rising inflation. Yet, the late 1970s saw high unemployment and *high* inflation, so-called stagflation. The period from 2013 to 2019 saw low unemployment and *low* inflation (inflation didn't really take off until 2021). So, where's the correlation? There isn't any. It's a fake theory with no empirical support. Still, the Fed swears by it. Is it any surprise that current monetary policy is driving the US economy over a cliff?

What do solid economic analysis and clear writing actually look like? They look like this book by Addison Wiggin. *The Demise of the Dollar* is a sterling example in the use of models that hold up in the real world and jargon-free exposition. This book is not only up-to-date and clear, it's an invaluable guide to navigating the uncharted economic waters that surround us.

To explain inflation, Addison does not need the Phillips curve. He simply compares prices of everyday goods like eggs, milk, and gas at the pump to what they cost a year or two years ago. That's the thing about inflation—you can't spin it. The price of food and fuel is in your face every day. You don't need a flawed model. You just have to watch your credit card balance go up and your savings account balance go down, and you'll know more about inflation than those trapped in an ivory tower at Harvard or in the West Wing.

Another great strength of his book is that Addison includes a heavy dose of history. Readers generally enjoy historical context for current events. History is like the spoonful of sugar that helps the economic medicine go down. Yet it's more than that. Inflation does not just drop out of the sky. It builds slowly through a succession of monetary policy blunders by the Federal Reserve and fiscal policy negligence by the Congress and White House. Addison takes us through the long litany of such blunders that has accrued over decades.

Addison looks at the creation of the Federal Reserve (1913), Bretton Woods (1944), the Marshall Plan (1948–1954), and Nixon's suspension of the convertibility of dollars for gold (1971) among other notable economic milestones. He explains why the United States and the world achieved strong growth and low inflation (1944–1971) followed by weak growth and high inflation (1971–1982), and then the Age of King Dollar (1983–2008) when the world learned to live without a gold standard but was utterly dependent on the Petrodollar standard.

Since 2008, we've encountered one crisis after another including financial panic, pandemic panic, supply chain breakdown, and now a full-scale shooting war in Europe with a financial war side-by-side. We abandoned solid economic policy in 1971 and are now reaping the bitter fruit of flawed policies ever since.

Best of all, Addison is not a doom-and-gloomer. He's forthright in his analysis and criticism but also positive in his recommendations. We are not victims. There are many ways to preserve wealth and even prosper in the most difficult economic times, and Addison lays these out clearly with specific recommendations for portfolio allocations and strategies.

I'm confident you will enjoy reading this book as much as I did. And I'm equally confident that you will come away from it with greater confidence in the future and a reliable playbook on how to survive.

ACKNOWLEDGMENTS

Writing a third edition of a book about a topic as big as the demise of the dollar is like hopping into a time machine. Looking back we got so many things right. The economic themes and trends have changed very little, except to get far more pronounced. We got a lot wrong, too, even with good intentions. It has been my own privilege to read the book again with a purpose. Not a lot of financial books make it to a third edition, especially 20 years after the first. It's an even greater privilege to rewrite and correct the ideas we discovered, either through history, or just experience, we believed strongly but ended up not happening at all. Studying the dollar as a free-floating currency among a sea of free-floating currencies and global politics is engaging, if nothing else. The second edition of the book was published in April 2008. So many of the themes we brought forward had to traverse the bailout period following the Panic of '08 and the great inflation during the pandemic years, 2020–2022.

During all this time I've been muttering to myself and anyone who'd listen about the consumer price index or "transitory inflation" or Bretton Woods. Mostly I was in my "uniform" for work, but during the pandemic, I spent days in, shall we say, "leisure attire" still thinking about the same things. All I can say is, *es lo que es*.

For all of that. . . I have to thank my wife, Jennifer, and my kids Henry, August, and Elizabeth. They've put up with me for long enough for the *Demise of the Dollar* to come out. (Wait until the next two!)

Jennifer, especially, has been as supportive of my career as anyone could hope for. Having been a publisher for two decades and now focusing on writing full time, the challenge is how much time I sit in a chair at the office in our home. Jennifer enters from time to time. She'll ask me about a unique dress she bought for a unique price or what day and time we ought to book our next flight. If I'm in the zone, I may end up staring at her, not understanding anything she's asking. On the other hand, I'll enter the kitchen trying to describe the impact of rising money supply on the gold price or what Triffin's paradox is. She'll likewise look at me with a smile that means something like "okay. . . ." It must be great fun being married to a writer. Or just annoying. Either way, I'm very grateful.

"Dad," Augie asked earlier this year, "do you know anything about the stock market?"

"I hope so," I replied wondering what he thought I'd been doing all his life. Augie's studying to be a veterinarian.

Liz has been dedicated to ballet since she was six years old and recently landed the lead in a production of *Cinderella*. I'd like to acknowledge that I did, in fact, fall asleep at that one recital. Okay, that other one too. And. . .well, you get the picture. She's a beautiful dancer.

Henry deserves a different kind of gratitude. He's the eldest of the three and has been doing research and writing for the book you hold in your hands. He's also been helping conceive and write editorials for our daily missive at *The Wiggin Sessions*. One of the facets I appreciate about Henry's work is the challenge he throws into my Gen X face. Growing up we used to challenge the morés of Baby Boomers. Now I know how they must have felt.

All three kids have thrown parties at different times that have gotten out of hand and caused a fair amount of mayhem. I'd like to acknowledge that they almost always turn the music down when we ask. Almost. They're good kids.

I'd be remiss if I didn't acknowledge Winston, the corgi puppy, who lives in our house. If he's not barking at the mailman, a squirrel, or the wind, he's usually sleeping within a couple of feet of me.

I would like to acknowledge two mentors who've helped guide and persuade me to do more, achieve more, be more. Thank you to Bill Bonner, my erstwhile writing partner. Thank you to Mark Ford, my erstwhile business coach. Both men have been very direct and instructive over the years. I appreciate every moment. The good. The bad. And the ugly.

Jim Rickards helped me to understand a couple of key concepts for this edition of the book. The supply side causes inflation versus the demand side. You'll learn more when you read. Jim also helped me parse the distinction between the US dollar as a reserve currency of the world and as a method of payment for the majority of Americans in their daily lives. Jim also makes a good lunch companion. You'll also note, Jim was kind enough to write the foreword to this edition.

I want to also thank fellow scrivener, Lawrence Sullivan, for the many off-hand discussions we've had about the writing process itself.

In my professional career, it would be hard not to thank just about everyone I've come into contact with. I've learned what to do—and what not to do—from everyone in a list of contacts that runs several minutes on my phone. The list is exactly why I started *The Wiggin Sessions* podcast. I've met some amazing, entrepreneurial, innovative, thoughtful, and talented people over the years. *The Wiggin Sessions* are a way to keep in touch. A way to say thank you. And a way to spread their good works. I've recorded more than 120 interviews, 100 of which are posted on YouTube and available by podcast. I've learned at least one solid new idea from each session. Sometimes more than that. The best way for me to acknowledge them all is to have you go ahead and check them out at *jointhesessions.com*.

The lockdown period of the pandemic created a period of rapid adaptation for all of us. With that idea in mind I'd like to thank the team who helped me envision and realize a plan to make it through. Judson Anglin, Kate Buck Jr., Itay Bengal, Mark O'Dell, Mia Blank, Henry Wiggin, Oscar Bejerano, Tyler Haynes and Russell Shea all contributed their unique talents to *The Wiggin Sessions,* allowing me to write and edit daily and work on this edition of *Demise*. Kate has been pushing for an upgrade to my own head space (and social presence) since 2017. It took a pandemic to make it happen. There's more to come!

Thank you, too, to Kevin Herrald, Susan Cerra, and Premkumar Narayanan at John Wiley & Sons for initiating this edition of *Demise of the Dollar*. Sheryl Nelson provided astute and thorough edits, helping to keep the story focused and alive for you if you're trying to understand the complexities of the dollar in your pocket.

INTRODUCTION

FISTFUL OF DOLLARS

December 15, 2022

Dear Reader,

We are living through a great inflation. It's why we feel pain at the pump, and why we grimace at the appalling price of a carton of eggs. It is also why the Fed is raising interest rates more aggressively than they have in half a century. And why if you want to buy a home or a car, you are forced to take out loans that are more and more expensive. And yet, most people just take out the loan, make the big purchase and buy, and deal with the consequences. The real question is: How long will the American consumer be able to sustain an ever-rising cost of living before they can no longer take it? And what does "not taking it anymore" really look like?

Historians will look back and say this inflationary period, 2020–2023, was on par with "The Great Inflation" of the 1970s. This period may even take the title. Whether you lived through the last great inflation, or are yet too young to understand what the country went through back then. . . this book is for you.

In fact, the book you are reading was not written for economists. Nor was it written for historians. This project began 20 years ago as a way to describe what is happening to the American dollar to everyday Americans.

In layman terms, the way you feel inflation is that everything seems more expensive. For example, every year the Farm Bureau calculates how much a traditional Thanksgiving home-cooked turkey dinner—turkey, mashed potatoes, corn casserole, the whole cornucopia—costs in comparison to the previous year. In the fall of 2022, the Farm Bureau estimated that the year's Thanksgiving dinner cost a total of $64.05, up $10.74 or 20% over 2021. The cost of dinner in 2021 had also increased by $6.41 or 14% over 2020. We only use "Thanksgiving dinner" as a metric because it is a thing everyone can grasp in some way. It's a metric economists use to see what matters to your budget and your family.

Let me pose a question: At what point does inflation become a problem for you? What would it take for you to, say, stop buying turkeys at all? And how do you solve it?

In old "Spaghetti Western" films—so named so because the films were made in Italy because it was cheaper to make them in Italy than in Hollywood—tales are told of men and women struggling in the American West to stay alive and maintain their freedoms. They had no money. They could only solve their problems using violence.

Today, wealth and prosperity has raised the standard of living far beyond those images of Clint Eastwood squinting at the old Mexican *bandito* across from him, quick to draw, quick to kill. Little remorse. Ashamed of what they have to do for a fistful of dollars. The tale of the American dollar is as old as the country itself. The modern details are not more complicated, except now we use computers instead of paper, and words instead of guns (most of the time). Today the bandits wear silk ties and look out over the Hudson River from their 40th floor suites.

There was a time when money was based on something real. People were willing to kill over it. Now, the dollar is worth less. . . or worthless. The demise of the dollar, in its simplest terms, is when the dollar means less and less over time. You might shake your fistful of dollars in anger at "the powers that be," that is if you even have enough bucks to muster. Our goal in this book is to help you under-stand what's happening behind the scenes so you don't have to shake your fist at all. . .you just have to make good decisions based on your understanding of how the dollar works today.

In fact, with all the division and derision spun in the media—on the television and on social media—the root cause of inflation is lost in the blender of political rhetoric. In turn, your ability to earn a living and how you take care of your family is as difficult as it has been in a half century.

A computer programmer might ask, "Is the American dollar more a feature or a bug?" Unfortunately, for the money in your wallet, the US dollar comes fully packaged with both. It is a feature that the US dollar is the reserve currency of the world. This means that every-body in the global economic system uses dollars for international trade and exchange. The US dollar has been the global reserve cur-rency since the end of the Second World War. When an oilman in Oslo, Norway, wants to ship his crude across the Atlantic to Rio de Janeiro, Brazil, the product is priced in dollars. That's the feature: The dollar is useful for international trade.

The dollar also comes equipped with a bug. When the international system gets out of whack, inflation sets in, and the prices rise for gas, chicken, cereal, clothes, shoes, toys—you name it. The American con-sumer is directly affected by international markets even if they don't know it. And that can be scary. Once you understand where inflation comes from, you can put yourself in the right position at the right time.

Is there any good news? You bet! There are steps that smart inves-tors can take now to escape from their vulnerability to the dollar's erratic price moves and its inevitable fall. This book lays out the problem of inflation and explains how we got here. It also explains how, with a properly positioned portfolio, the demise of the dollar could actually be beneficial to your finances.

"Where should I put my money, Wiggin?" readers ask on my pod-cast regularly. Read on. We will provide you with the specifics about what's really going on with the dollar and our economy, why the American consumer is addicted to spending beyond their means, and how foreign countries ultimately control our economic fate. Finally, we offer strategies you can put into action today to not only protect your financial freedom but to thrive in an economic downturn, and even in a crisis.

The *Demise of the Dollar* is and has been an ongoing investigation since its inception in 2004. *Demise* follows the rise and fall, the pride and prejudice, of the American dollar. We've also written books about the booms and busts in economic cycles in *Financial Reckoning Day*, and the political follies that have led to such exorbitant and foolhardy decisions and policies, that have led to annual deficits mounting national debt and political debauchery at the federal level in *Empire of Debt*.

When we began this project in 2004, big economic words like "bailouts," "negative interest rates," and "cryptocurrencies" hadn't yet entered the financial conversation. Now it seems like it is all we talk about. We are fortunate to have been engaged in this project long enough that we can incorporate these new terms into our narrative and help you understand what's going on with your own fistful of dollars.

Many of the ideas in this, the third edition, of the book have been updated based on discussions I've had in *The Wiggin Sessions*, a podcast I conceived during a tornado warning late one Friday afternoon in downtown Baltimore. The tornado warning was rare enough, but we were already on lockdown during the COVID-19 pandemic. A colleague and I cracked open a bottle of wine and started taking notes on a white board. *The Wiggin Sessions* were born. I have been conducting interviews with hundreds of people since. Most are the people I have met during my three decade career in the financial publishing industry. We've been posting them to YouTube and on social media.

What I have discovered while doing these podcasts is there is a far greater need for understanding of the basic economic principles that govern our daily lives than what I originally thought. I've learned there's a danger of assuming I know what you, as a reader, are already aware of and what I think is helpful for you to know. There's a divide. Social media and the fact that people don't really read books anymore, at least not in their entirety, makes the mission to communicate even more sacrosanct.

While writing and editing the third edition of *Demise of the Dollar*, I discovered there were some concepts I got wrong in the first and second editions. Perfectionist that I am, in this third edition I am attempting to not only correct those first misconceptions but also help readers to understand how the economy and the value of the dollar—the currency itself—has been changing so rapidly in our life-times. Without getting too ontological, I do want to comment on the very fact of being right or wrong in this field called *economics*. A lot of the time people "on both sides of the aisle" like to throw the hot potato back and forth, pointing fingers, playing the blame-game, or whatever you want to call it. That's just not how it works, frankly, in the markets or in life (and money and the economy, whether we like it or not, is a metaphor for our lives). So in reading my words, please take my storytelling with the necessary grain of salt. If anything, it's an epic story. Enjoy.

—Addison Scott Wiggin
Baltimore, Maryland 2022

CHAPTER 1

THE GREENBACK BOOGIE

See the money, wanna stay for your meal.
Get another piece of pie, for your wife

—Ima Robot (Suits theme)

Our way in is through "inflation." Most people think inflation is when things get more expensive. But what if we thought something different? What if we changed our definition of inflation and thought of rising prices as *the result*, not the definition?

It is simple economics, actually. The more that you have of something, the less value it has. Think: if I had the one and only baseball card of Carl Yastrzemski, it would be worth a lot on the sports memorabilia market. If everyone had a Carl Yastrzemski card, mine wouldn't matter at all. The analogy fits for me because I grew up in New England. Carl Yastrzesmski was a famous first baseman for the Boston Red Sox when I was a kid. Baseball cards were a thing too. A Yastrzemski card when you opened the bubble gum pack and got one, euphoria. It was, like, "Whoa, what, seriously? A Yastrzemski card?!"

One card means a lot. But if there were thousands of them. Billions or trillions of them. You get the point. The same thing goes for the American dollar bill. Substitute the Yastrzemski card with "the American greenback" and the more dollars you have in the system, the less each dollar is worth. And today, those "dollars" are created by digits.

What this means to the consumer—you and me—is that the dollar doesn't go as far. The items we want to buy feel more expensive. This is because you need more dollars to buy the things you want. But are things really more expensive? Or is the dollar just worth less because there are more of them in the system? It can be confusing! And around and around we go. That's why we call it the "greenback boogie." We're going to explain what that means.

The essential value of the American dollar itself is and has been in question. It's a feature of the economic system in which we live. The dollar is what's in your wallets, so it could present you with a big problem. What if we all start worrying about food on the table, our mortgages, taxes, retirement, tuition, gas for our commutes to work, and the cost of weddings and marriages and vacations, all at the same time? In the end, without what we call "sound money"—money whose value we can rely on—it is really hard to figure out if you have the right amount of money and whether the financial decisions you are making actually work. It doesn't really matter what currency you spend your money in. It's whether you can trust what you earn your money in and whether that money is going to be worth anything when you want to buy something.

In earlier editions of the book, we were forecasting inflation. During the pandemic and now, as the economy begins opening up, inflation—rising prices—is in our face. In 2022, we began to really think about the phenomenon that we call "inflation" and what we can do to manage our money through it.

THAT WHICH IS SEEN

Economists often look to the French philosopher Frédéric Bastiat's "Parable of the Broken Window" for guidance on how to conduct an economic study. He says with all things there is always "that which is seen, and that which is not seen." The idea is very helpful when trying to understand the economy and the stock market at large and, further, the problem of inflation and the effect it has on the money in your wallet. Bastiat writes:

> In the department of economy, an act, a habit, an institution, a law, gives birth not only to an effect, but to a series of effects. Of these

effects, the first only is immediate; it manifests itself simultaneously with its cause—*it is seen*. The others unfold in succession—*they are not seen*: it is well for us if they are *foreseen*. Between a good and a bad economist this constitutes the whole difference—the one takes account of the *visible* effect; the other takes account both of the effects which are *seen* and also of those which it is necessary to *foresee*.

What is seen is the chairman of the Federal Reserve—currently Jerome Powell—announcing on television to the American people that he and his Federal Open Markets Committee (FOMC)—the policy-deciding wing of the Fed—are raising interest rates yet again to tackle a so-called "transitory inflation." Pulses quicken. Mortgage rates go up. Credit cards are harder to pay off.

In 2021–22, we saw a sea change in interest rate hikes. In a very short amount of time, the rate you needed to pay for a mortgage, home equity loan, or tuition payments increased by the quickest pace ever induced by the Federal Reserve. (See Figure 1.1)

Most people don't know that interest rates determine the rate you have to pay on your credit cards and mortgages. You want to buy a house, you will have to take out a mortgage loan (unless you can pay up front). The interest rate at which you borrow for your mortgage loan is usually around "a point" above the rate decided by the FOMC.

Whether you like it or not, Jerome Powell and his posse are making decisions that directly affect you as an investor and consumer. As the head of the central bank of the United States—colloquially dubbed "the Fed"—Powell announces the collective decision of

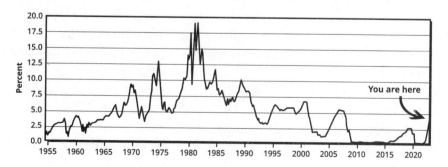

FIGURE 1.1 Federal Funds Effective Rate, 1955–2020
(Source: Board of Governors of the Federal Reserve System (US))

America's seven central bank governors. All together, the committee sets the interest rate for the American banking system. Which, as we all know, is priced in American dollars.

They call it the "overnight Fed funds rate." And the financial media, yours truly included, have taken to "Fed-watching," as we call it, in the last two years. We hang onto every word issued by Powell and the FOMC because it determines the very value of our dollars. Your money.

"What have they decided?" journalists want to know.

"What does it mean?' we ask.

"Can we still buy homes without going bankrupt?" everyone and their mother worries. Then the keyboards get to clacking.

To reiterate: we see the headlines and the analysis of the Fed's every interest rate manipulation. What we don't see: Jerome Powell's actions are actually the culmination of more than three decades of Federal Reserve trials in economic theory.

You might still be thinking: "Why the hell should I care about what the Federal Reserve does to interest rates? I've got better things to do." To which I will respond: In trying to manage the American banking system, the Federal Reserve and the FOMC are directly influencing the value of the money in your wallet. When they tug at strings from up top, you feel it in your wallet.

The Federal Reserve governors think they can manipulate the value of the dollar by lowering and raising rates based on signals from the 12 banks in the American Reserve bank system. This is what we call "the greenback boogie." It's a jazz beat. And it's confusing as it sounds. All the world's a stage to the Fed's two-step. But why? It hasn't always been this way. We haven't always been doing the greenback boogie. In fact, the Federal Reserve didn't always determine the value of the dollar, nor did it always manipulate the dollar in an attempt to regulate its ups and downs.

For 23 years—between 1944 and 1971—the dollar was "pegged to gold." That simply means that the gold price on the world market determined what the dollar could be redeemed for by other countries holding assets priced in dollars. The nation's central bank, the Federal Reserve, did not try to control the value of the dollar through interest rate adjustment as they do today. In 1971, what's called the "gold standard" for the US dollar was disbanded. Then the story changed, and the boogie began.

In the story of how we got here, there's a cast of characters. The protagonists are involved in complex discussions about how to organize the global economy and its currency system at the end of World War II, a war that destroyed most of Europe, Western Russia, and the Southeast Pacific. Let's begin.

WELCOME TO BRETTON WOODS

Our story begins in a little town in New Hampshire on July 1, 1944. For the first time in modern history, an international agreement was reached to govern monetary policy among the world's nations. It was a chance to create a stable international currency once and for all. In total, 730 delegates from 44 nations met for three weeks at a resort in Bretton Woods.

The conference was held at the Mount Washington Hotel in the shadows of the largest mountain in the Granite State, Mount Washington. Mount Washington is known for some of the most severe weather in the lower 48 contiguous states. Seems all too fitting a location for a conference discussing what to do with the world's money as the closing battles of World War II raged on in Europe and the South Pacific.

The hotel itself was, and still is, as ostentatious and grand as the aims of the 44 countries who sent their delegates.

The economist John Maynard Keynes led the British delegation—he was something of an economic superstar because of his academic prowess and access to the government ruling class in Great Britain. He was a member of the famous Bloomsbury Group, friends with a hip crowd of writers like Virginia Wolfe and E.M. Forster. He also argued that governments needed to expand their power in typical "Progressive fashion." Think Steven Pinker or Yuval Noah Harari, but back in the day.

Harry Dexter White led the United States' efforts. (As a side note to the history we are building for you, in 1948 Harry Dexter White was accused of being a Russian spy during the war and through the conference. Later declassified Russian documents further added to the cloud of suspicion overhanging the formerly high ranking US

(Source: https://en.wikipedia.org/wiki/Mount_Washington_Hotel)

Treasury official.) France, Mexico, and the British Commonwealths like Canada, Australia, and New Zealand also attended. Brazil and 36 other Allied countries sent diplomats and economists. The Soviet Union even joined the conference, although in the end they didn't register a vote.[1]

Bretton Woods presented a significant opportunity for the global economic community. But like all diplomatic efforts of this size and scope, it fell short of what could have been achieved. It was, however, a turning point in monetary history.

The intended purpose of the meeting was to discuss ideas both Keynes and White had been working on since early in the Second World War. Without discounting the world's tragic casualties, it was clear early enough in the conflict that the global economy would be destroyed and, after the smoke cleared and the peace treaties were signed, would need to be rebuilt from the ground up, both literally and metaphorically.

In some respects, Bretton Woods was a lot like an economic United Nations. The combination of the Great Depression of the 1930s and the Second World War required a global economic summit of unprecedented magnitude.

The consensus of the delegates was that trade barriers and high costs had caused the worldwide depression, at least in part. Also, during that time it was common practice to use currency devaluation as a means of affecting neighboring countries' imports and reducing payment deficits. Unfortunately, the practice led to chronic deflation, unemployment, and a reduction in international trade. The situation was summed up well by Cordell Hull, U.S. Secretary of State from 1933 through 1944, who wrote:

> Unhampered trade dovetailed with peace; high tariffs, trade barriers, and unfair economic competition, with war. . . . If we could get a freer flow of trade . . . so that one country would not be deadly jealous of another and the living standards of all countries might rise, thereby eliminating the economic dissatisfaction that breeds war, we might have a reasonable chance of lasting peace.

Hull's suggestion that war often has an economic root is reasonable given the position of both Germany and Japan in the 1930s. Many historians believe Japan's sneak attack on Pearl Harbor, "a day that will live in infamy," was forced by a trade embargo imposed by the United States against Japan. Another observer agreed, saying poor economic relations among nations "inevitably result in economic warfare that will be but a prelude and instigator of military warfare on an even vaster scale."

The solution to such crooked manipulation of money? A worldwide agreement. Easier said than done. Keynes preferred establishing a system that would have encouraged economic growth rather than a gold-pegged system. He favored the creation of an international central bank and possibly even a world currency backed by a "basket of commodities" and proposed that the goal of the conference was "to find a common measure, a common standard, a common rule acceptable to each and not irksome to any."

Keynes's ideas were not accepted. The United States preferred the plan offered by its representative, Harry Dexter White. The US position was intended to create and maintain price stability rather than Keynes's supposed economic growth.

At the end of the Second World War, the United States had more gold than anyone else: 70% of the world's gold reserves.[2] That will be an important detail in 23 years. Due to this perceived economic dominance, the United States held the leadership role at Bretton Woods. And like in many situations, he who holds the gold wins the argument. The amount of gold held in reserve is going to be important when we get to the political reason to end the Bretton Woods Agreement and take the dollar off the gold standard, so keep that in mind.

The official Bretton Woods Agreement laid out a plan for international monetary policy based on a global gold standard. By "pegging" their currencies to the U.S. dollar, which was in turn "pegged" to gold, each country signing the accord promised to maintain its currency at values at or close to the value of gold. In addition, the International Monetary Fund (IMF) was established to facilitate payment imbalances on a temporary basis. The system devised during the conference was bureaucratic in nature; the newly established International Bank for Reconstruction and Development (IBRD, now the World Bank) and the IMF were created and funded, along with a series of infrastructure loans to war-ravaged nations.

In an ominous statement released by President in 1953, it is apparent that the political aims of the IMF began under shoddy leadership. Truman said:

> It was originally planned that the United States would support Mr. White for election to the top managerial position in the International Monetary Fund—that of managing director—a more important post than that of a member of the board of executive directors. But following the receipt of the FBI report and the consultations with members of my Cabinet, it was decided that he would be limited to membership on the board of directors. With his duties thus restricted, he would be subject to the supervision of the Secretary of State, and his position would be less important and much less sensitive—if it were sensitive at all—than the position then held by him as Assistant Secretary of the Treasury.

As a consequence, the progress of emerging economies would be achieved through lending and infrastructure investment through the IMF, but without Dexter White at its head. In joining the IMF, each country was assigned a trade quota to fund the international effort, budgeted originally at $8.8 billion. Disparity among countries was to be managed through a series of borrowings. A country could borrow from the IMF, which would be acting in fact like a central bank.

The IMF and the World Bank exist right now and appear in the news on a regular basis. They are the pillars of the global economic economy to this day. They are a big piece of the puzzle of inflation and the demise of the dollar, but there's more to the story of Bretton Woods.

WHAT IS "THE GOLD STANDARD"?

Throughout most of the nineteenth century, the "gold standard" dominated currency exchange. The Bretton Woods system attempted to recreate a Victorian-era monetary policy of a similar nature—namely, the British pound being pegged directly to gold. Gold created a fixed exchange rate between nations. Money supply was limited to gold reserves. In this way, the currency was stable and could not be manipulated by central banks. It's what has been referred to since as "sound money."

The gold standard established by the Bretton Woods Agreement worked for 25 years. It's a short amount of time, even when measured against the 234 years the United States has been a country. The peg of the US dollar to gold maintained sensible economic policy based on a nation's gold reserves.

In theory, gold became the method of guaranteeing the value of a currency. A productive nation under this exchange rate system was one that could trade favorably and confidently. Following Bretton Woods, the pegged rate was formalized by agreement among the leading economic powers of the world.

But it was flawed in its underlying assumptions. The concept was a good one. In practice, however, the international currency naturally became the US dollar, and other nations pegged their currencies to the dollar rather than to the value of gold.

So what happened?

The actual outcome of Bretton Woods was to replace the gold standard with a gold standard that depended on the US dollar. The

United States linked the dollar to gold at a value of $35 per ounce. By pegging international currency to gold at $35 an ounce, it failed to take into consideration the change in gold's actual value since 1934, when the $35 level had been set. This disconnect was the beginning of the demise of the dollar.

This problem was described by a senior vice president of the Federal Reserve Bank of New York:

> From the very beginning, gold was the vulnerable point of the Bretton Woods system. Yet the open-ended gold commitment assumed by the United States government under the Bretton Woods legislation is readily understandable in view of the extraordinary circumstances of the time.
>
> At the end of the war, our gold stock amounted to $20 billion, roughly 60 percent of the total of official gold reserves. As late as 1957, United States gold reserves exceeded by a ratio of three to one the total dollar reserves of all the foreign central banks. The dollar bestrode the exchange markets like a colossus.

As well-intentioned as the idea was, the agreements and institutions that grew from Bretton Woods were not adequate for the economic problems of postwar Europe. The United States was experiencing huge trade surplus years while carrying European war debt. US reserves were huge and growing each year.

By 1947, it became clear that the IMF and IBRD were not going to fix Europe's problems after the Second World War. To help address the issue, the United States set up a system to help finance recovery among European countries. The European Recovery Program (better known as the Marshall Plan) was organized to give grants to countries to rebuild. The problems of European nations, according to Secretary of State George Marshall, "are so much greater than her present ability to pay that she must have substantial help or face economic, social, and political deterioration of a very grave character."

Between 1948 and 1954, the United States gave 16 Western European nations $17 billion in grants. Believing that former enemies Japan and Germany would provide markets for future US exports, policies were enacted to encourage economic growth.

It became increasingly difficult to maintain the peg of the US dollar to $35-per-ounce gold. An open market in gold continued in London, and crises began to affect the going-value of gold. The conflict between the fixed price of gold between central banks at $35 per ounce and open market value worsened. During the Cuban Missile Crisis in 1962, for example, the open market value of gold was $40 per ounce. The mood among US leaders began moving away from belief in the gold standard and straining the Bretton Woods Agreement. President Lyndon B. Johnson argued in 1967:

> The world supply of gold is insufficient to make the present system workable—particularly as the use of the dollar as a reserve currency is essential to create the required international liquidity to sustain world trade and growth.[3]

It became apparent that the idea of progress could not be funded by gold alone. On March 17, 1968, a run on gold closed the London Gold Pool permanently. Maintaining the gold standard under the Bretton Woods configuration was no longer practical for the political agendas of the day. Either the monetary system had to change or the gold standard itself would need to be revised.

In a last ditch effort to keep the Bretton Woods Agreement afloat, the IMF set up Special Drawing Rights (SDRs) for use as trade between countries. The intention was to create a type of paper-gold hybrid system, while taking pressure off the United States to continue serving as central banker to the world. However, this did not solve the problem; the depletion of US gold reserves continued until 1971. The United States held only 22% gold coverage of foreign reserves by that year.

Bretton Woods lacked any effective mechanism for checking reserve growth. Nobody knew who had the actual, physical gold. Only American dollars were considered seriously as reserves, and gold production was lagging. Accordingly, dollar reserves had to expand to make up the difference in lagging gold availability.

Bretton Woods ceased to function as an effective centralized monetary body. In theory, SDRs—used today on a very limited scale of transactions between the IMF and its members—could function as the beginnings of an international currency. But given the widespread use of the US dollar as the peg for so many currencies worldwide, it is unlikely that such a shift to a new direction will occur before circumstances make it the only choice.

Finally the problem fell on another man's shoulders. In 1971, experiencing rapidly accelerating depletion of its gold reserves, President Richard "Tricky Dick" Nixon and the United States removed its currency from the "gold standard," and the Bretton Woods Agreement was no longer in effect.

He famously blamed it on speculators betting against the US dollar itself, but it was the depletion of gold reserves that really got everyone spooked. If the US dollar was pegged to gold reserves, and those gold reserves were depleting, well, then, the gig would be up.

The only solution at the point would have been to end the peg.

CHAPTER 2

"WE ARE ALL KEYNESIANS NOW"

My baby gives me the finance blues,
Tax me to the limit of my revenues.

—The Grateful Dead

It was the end of an era. The demise of the dollar began with what is tantamount to an international margin call—and even the most unsophisticated investor knows the words "margin" and "call" are bad when put together in one phrase. Simply put, your guy at the brokerage firm calls to tell you that your assets are in trouble. You've got two choices: either deposit more money into your account, or sell off one of your assets to stay afloat. If you don't have more money to put in. . .well, you can do the math yourself.

On August 15, 1971, the United States didn't have the gold reserves it said it had. And it was worried that it would have less even sooner.[1]

The French president at the time, Charles de Gaulle, wanted gold, not American dollars. De Gaulle recognized the Johnson administration was trying to fight two wars at one time: the Vietnam War in Southeast Asia and "the War on Poverty" at home. Maybe he'd had some insight since the French defeat at Dien Bien Phu in 1954.

Wars are expensive. So are social policies. The United States was running up deficits. In turn, the dollar was getting less valuable. De Gualle recognized it was for political decisions, not because of some intrinsic economic phenomena. Economic history shows us that governments get emboldened to spend more than their currency can handle.

One can almost imagine de Gaulle saying in a thick French accent, "I'm not going to support the policies, so I will take the gold." Those were the terms of the Bretton Woods Agreement.

If the United States would continue to be the dominant Western economy, then it would also have to be good stewards of its own money.

De Gaulle referred to the Bretton Woods exchange rate system as a *"privilège exorbitant"* that gave the United States a substantial advantage in the global economy. Barry Eichengreen writes that the world under Bretton Woods was an "asymmetric financial system" in his book *Exorbitant Privilege.* The French found "themselves supporting American living standards and subsidizing American multinationals.'" *Time* magazine too reported in 1965:

> Treasury Secretary Douglas Dillon made the first public admission that the U.S. payments deficit in 1964 moved higher than anyone had expected. It totaled about $3 billion, all of which the U.S. is legally committed to exchange for U.S. gold on demand. The Federal Reserve announced that the U.S. gold supply declined last week by $100 million, to a 26-year low of $15.1 billion.
>
> Under a gold standard the U.S. would no longer be able to pay its foreign debts in dollars, but only in gold. U.S. businessmen would have to curtail their investments in foreign companies. (De Gaulle last week called such U.S. investments "a form of expropriation").[2]

President de Gaulle recognized that the global monetary system was rigged against the French franc, even if they were allies in the war. By 1968, de Gaulle had pulled the French out of the London Gold Pool in an effort to exchange francs for gold directly.

PRIVILÈGE REVOKED

We can look at gold in a couple of ways: as the basis for solid asset value or as a tangible investment with its own supply and demand market. Many people today shy away from gold because of the incredible price movement between 1971 and 1980. This occurred following two important and critical events.

In 1971, President Nixon took the United States off the gold standard (meaning we could print as much money as we want, right?). And then in 1974, President Gerald Ford removed a 40-year-old restriction on Americans' right to own gold.

Looking back to 1933, the Great Depression caused a serious gold shortage. The Emergency Banking Relief Act of 1933 was passed "to provide relief in the existing national emergency in banking and for other purposes. . . ."[3]

The bill required all citizens to turn over gold coin and currency in exchange for Federal Reserve notes. Refusing to turn over gold carried a $10,000 fine and 10 years in jail. This unusual move was intended to prevent the public from hoarding gold bullion. The solution was a simple one: make it illegal to own gold directly. But as is often the case when a government acts under emergency powers, this critical law started the ball rolling toward the trouble our dollar is in today.

Once Nixon dismantled the Bretton Woods system effectively ending the post-war gold standard and Ford removed the restriction on owning gold, the price shot up from the regulated $35 per ounce. It topped out above $800 by January 1980. Adjusted for inflation, that's $2,499 in 2022 dollars. And remains gold's highest historical price. By 1999, it had dropped to $235. In 2012, following the bailout period gold returned to $2,308. Then during the mid-pandemic month of August 2020, gold returned again to $2,250. For now, we should not look at gold price gyrations as a market-driven phenomenon. The climb and subsequent fall and dramatic rise again and then again were caused by government intervention over a 40-year period. Here are four compelling arguments:

1. *The trade gap.* The US trade surplus of years ago disappeared in 1977 never to return. After years of strong surplus in trade, it all changed only six years after the removal of the gold standard. Here's what is troubling about all of this: Because the Fed is free to decide how much money to print up, it means that our ever-growing IOUs are becoming worth less and less. We buy more and more on credit, and our IOUs are

piling up. The days when currency was backed by gold are gone, and the United States has become a riverboat gambler, drunk and losing, demanding more and more credit to continue playing. Let's not overlook the historical reality: When the dollar's value falls, gold's value rises. As our trade deficit gets ever higher and as the Fed continues printing IOUs, the value begins to soften. The more currency put into circulation, the greater the dilution and the worse the situation becomes. But as we've seen, for the price of gold, this is good news.

2. *The budget deficit.* Where is the government getting all of that money it continues to spend? The $1.4 trillion budget deficit in the bailout year 2009 depended on the incredibly low interest rates that have been the centerpiece of the Fed's monetary policy since the financial crisis. Over the next decade, the best Congress could do was spend $441 billion more than they brought in. That number, achieved in 2015, would have been horrifying itself before the bailouts. It only gets worse from there. During the pandemic year of 2020 the government ran a deficit of $3.1 trillion. The numbers are so big they don't bother anyone anymore. New academic theories, like the Modern Monetary Theory, have arisen to justify—even encourage—their existence. Still, even in 2020, low interest rates accommodated these nosebleed deficits. But, we hesitate to ask, what happens when rates start to climb as they did in earnest in 2022 as the Fed sought to "fight" inflation? Remember, inflation is a measure of the number of IOUs in the economy. Each year's budget deficit only adds more IOUs, adds to the national debt, and further fuels inflation. The budget itself sinks deeper and deeper into the hole. Who is going to make those interest payments in the future? The higher the debt, the higher the interest. And the higher the interest rate, the greater the impact on the taxpayer—you and me and our children. It's called "crowding out": more taxes must go toward interest payments leaving less room for spending on the government programs politicians have promised. The math is not encouraging.

3. *A limited world supply.* Gold is a limited commodity, unlike currency. As long as the Fed has access to printing presses, it is able to continue pumping adrenaline into the economy. But gold is real money in every sense, and its value is enhanced because there is only so much of it. This is the most important difference between currency and money. Now that we are off the gold standard, the Fed believes it can ignore currency valuation and continue on the "full faith and credit" system. As an investment, the dollar is becoming more and more suspect. In comparison, as dollar troubles get worse, the limited supply of gold will become more valuable. Cause and effect—that is what drives market values. Dollars fall; gold rises. It's unavoidable.

4. *The currency value of gold.* Most people can appreciate the difference between an IOU and actual money. If your boss handed you an IOU on payday, you would not be happy. You'd rather be able to cash a check and use the money. But in fact, the dollar is an IOU, and we're all trading these IOUs as currency without any real backing. We are going to see an increasing trend among foreign central banks to buy gold in exchange for dollars, as they did following the Russian invasion of Ukraine. This gradually increasing demand for gold will have the unavoidable impact of increasing gold's market value. How high can it go? Only time will tell, but the weakening dollar is encouraging for gold investors.

Back in 1971, if Nixon had removed the restriction on gold value at $35 an ounce and allowed it to find its value in the open market, that would have done more to fix the international monetary problem. But removing the restriction on gold value was not considered a viable option, for two reasons:

First, it would have meant the United States was telling other countries (those with undervalued currencies) to raise their prices on exports to the United States. And that would never have gone over well in countries that, at the time, were being subsidized by the US dollar, economically speaking.

Second, the change would have drastically affected world markets of natural resources, including oil—doubling the barrel price of oil.

That would not have gone over well, either—although a few years later, we did in fact experience double-digit inflation and long lines at the pump as a consequence of going off the gold standard.

Nixon's decision was viewed as the only alternative to devaluing the dollar. Currency markets already recognized that US dollars had been inflated. In December 1971, leaders of the so-called Group of Ten industrialized nations met in Washington, DC, to officially change currency values based on the per-ounce value of gold raised from $35 to $38. The dollar was lowered 7.89%, while the German mark was raised 13.57%, and the Japanese yen went up 16.9%.

Removing the US dollar from the Bretton Woods system was an attempt at solving the problem of falling currencies overseas. The currency exchange between US dollars and European and Japanese currencies was a drain on US trade. This is *opposite* to the problem we face today: The dollar is falling for those who use it, meaning what you want to buy gets more expensive. But the dollar is also gaining value against other currencies in the world as a way to settle trade accounts. It can be confusing. Confusing is the nature of the fiat system.

President Nixon's own admission when he signed the act that ended the Bretton Woods exchange rate system was historic. "We're all Keyensians now," referring to the idea that even those who had politically supported free market initiatives a la Mises and Hayek were giving in to political incentives. Nixon appears beaten in the films of the episode. Perhaps, because of years of championing, at least while campaigning for office, the old right idea of less government intervention in the economy, fewer taxes, more individual freedom. As a student of history, and irony, it's outstanding how great and offensive the Nixon administration was. Studying the era is also perplexing. We're constantly reminded of Lord Acton's comment that "absolute power corrupts absolutely." It's even worse when your goal is just power for its own sake. At least Acton was critiquing monarchies. In monarchies there is meant to be a God-given grant to power. In democracies, or republics like the United States, you have to get gritty. It's not pretty.

Of course, the wage and price controls of the Nixon era did not work. Yes, Nixon won reelection in 1972, but unemployment did not fall, and inflation did not go away (in fact, it got worse). The administration reimposed the freeze controls that had failed before, then quietly canceled them in April 1974, only four months before Nixon resigned. By then, unfortunately, the unavoidable expansion in inflation, unemployment, and a falling dollar had begun.[4]

We have to remember the meaning of the dollar's peg to gold and why it served such an important role in international economic policy. The gold standard was a means by which countries agreed to fix the value of their currency, based on amounts of gold reserves. The abandonment of the gold standard during World War I when most countries involved in the fighting financed their war effort with inflationary money—IOUs—eventually contributed to the massive devaluation in the 1920s and worldwide depression of the 1930s. We should learn from history. Abandoning the gold standard devastates the world economy. Let's watch what happens from there.

FULL FAITH AND CREDIT

The US monetary system, and by extension that of the global monetary system, as well, reverted to one of "fiat money"—a system in which the government dictates the value of a currency rather than pegging it to the value of gold (or other precious metal) reserves. The decision was the beginning of what we call the Great Dollar Standard Era: the moment the American greenback was no longer backed by gold. It was henceforth backed by the "full faith and credit of the US government." The Federal Reserve, a private bank, is the steward of that full faith and credit.

Mostly, we don't carry them anymore, but if, in fact, you do have a dollar in your wallet, you'll see it is simply a promissory note. Check what it says at the top of the bill itself: "Federal Reserve Note." The American dollars in circulation are all just a bunch of IOUs. That would be fine if gold reserves were sitting tight in Fort Knox to back them up. . . but they are not. The value of the dollar is floating. "Floating on what?" you might ask. And you'd be right to ask.

Prior to 1971, most of the world's currencies were backed by gold because they were pegged to the US dollar. The dollar was redeemable in gold.

We know that supply and demand alter the value of every commodity in an efficient economic system. As demand increases for a unit of exchange, the price rises. This is an efficient system. Demand pushes the price up, and supply pushes the price down.

When paper money is in use, the whole efficiency of the economic system goes out the window. As long as the government can print more money, it can continue to expand a consumption base in spite of any supply and demand, and in spite of the limited supply of gold itself. Again, we're not arguing for gold as a base for value. We're not ones to argue against history either. Gold has been used as money for a lot longer than the dollar. Or Bitcoin, for that matter.

Let's just be clear. The Fed and Treasury keep printing money. In what space of history will that not catch up with them? We could name names, but does that matter? It's a systemic issue. Who even asks these people what they're up to? The day will come when "we" will have to pay off those IOUs.

As we like to point out in *The Wiggin Sessions,* the gold standard was a useful and important economic tool. The fact that gold existed only in limited supply meant that governments could not simply print all the money they wanted to, regardless of the political challenge or ambition.

So what went wrong? Why did Richard Nixon dismantle the Bretton Woods exchange rate system? And why was it perhaps the greatest mistake in the history of American money? The whole basis for money itself—currency as a means of exchange—is based on tangible value. Without getting too philosophical, the value of your money is not the green bills we carry around, or the digits we have on our credit cards; it's a matter of trust.

Before I write this next statement I would like to assert that I'm not a "gold bug." Gold has been money for thousands of years. No fiat money system has ever succeeded, which we'll see later. History has shown time and again that excessive government spending eventually makes paper money worthless. But that doesn't have to mean that gold is the end all of your financial picture. Our purpose here is to understand why fiat money has failed historically.

We'll admit. An argument against the gold standard is based on gold's rarity. You can't fight wars on the gold standard, for example.

Nor can you expand the economy of credit and speculation. We cannot expect any economic expansion as long as we are held back by a commodity in limited supply, the argument goes.

So then you get banking without borders. Money is not "printed" anymore. It's just digits moved from one screen to another. Money without borders, without restraint, eventually, exceeds its own life cycle. It becomes worthless, as we have seen time and again—in Rome, China, Spain, France, Germany, and now the United States. Why do we still believe it can work?

The fiat money system in effect in the United States today makes this point. It may be interesting to note that today many economists fear that a return to the gold standard or institution of an international monetary system could actually trigger a depression—a collapse of the financial economy. It is no simple matter to revert to a more sensible standard. Consequences are inevitable.

It would not be easy for the major currencies to return to an organized Bretton Woods exchange rate system. The growth that occurred in the post–World War II era is possible. It can only happen with money that is outside the political system. (Yes, we'll talk about Bitcoin and cryptocurrencies later in the book.)

The official reason for dismantling the Bretton Woods exchange rate system going off the gold standard was relatively simple: to stop dollar speculators and encourage US trade partners to peg their currencies directly to the US dollar without the dollar peg to gold; in other words, it was an attempt at getting foreign governments to realign their currency values and trust in the full faith and credit of the US government. Why? Nixon recognized that relying on gold as settlement for international exchange of goods and services inhibited expansion of the US economy and the US outsized share of above ground gold was rapidly dwindling.

If we recognize that currency is simply a form of IOU—literally "I owe you"—against the value of goods and services we exchange, then we can see why the tables have turned.

In 1971, the major foreign currencies were devalued against the dollar and gold. The abandonment of the gold standard had a far deeper and longer-lasting effect than the inflationary adjustments of the 1970s. Why? Because our "money approximate" dollar circulated based on commodity reserves (gold and silver). That went away.

Nixon was concerned that the gold standard inhibited our ability to compete with devalued currencies in other nations. The US government was known to issue currency above reserves by speculating, offsetting long positions in dollars with short positions in gold, and gambling that it was unlikely that demands would be made against currency reserves. But that's exactly what happened. In the days before Nixon's decision, the British ambassador presented a demand for conversion of $3 billion in currency into gold.

When Nixon dismantled the Bretton Woods exchange rate system, he also tried to stabilize the economy with a series of ill-fated price controls. Historically, these government controls are known as the "Nixon Shock." He wanted to curb the inflation kicked off in 1965 by massive government spending intended to support President Johnson's Great Society. By 1971, inflation was increasing. For the first time in the post-war period, everyday Americans actually worried about what inflation might do to their net worth or their ability to buy the things they wanted at a reasonable price, much as today. Think 5%–6% interest rates are bad? Think 13%–14%.

Listening to his Fed chairman, then Arthur Burns, Nixon believed what he'd been told: that the traditional view of money was wrong and the key to economic recovery was government control over prices and wages.

The misguided belief that wage and price controls would fix the economy by reducing inflation and creating new jobs turned out to be, well, wrong—not to mention an affront to Nixon's Republican principles that were supposed to favor a free market. The decision to impose controls was part of a plan to stimulate new employment in time for the 1972 presidential election. Burns warned Nixon that going off the gold standard would be viewed in Moscow and in the Russian press—at the height of the Cold War—as a bad sign for the United States. He warned, "*Pravda* would write that this was a sign of the collapse of capitalism. It's a curiosity of history that government controls were meant to preserve the free market. And, theoretically an antidote to the government controlled economy of the US' Cold War foe, the USSR.

Thankfully, while it has taken more than 50 years for the evidence to present itself fully, the decisions made by Nixon in 1971 set the process in motion. Capitalism as it was did not collapse immediately.

The concept of a free and open market is challenged in one important respect today: The US dollar's value is falling for everyday Americans and remains a question mark in the eyes of foreign banks and investors who use it as a store of value. There is also much trepidation about the rising second largest economy in the world, China. There is also concerns caused by the sanctions imposed on Russia following the invasion of Ukraine. The Russians would rather not use the dollar as a pricing tool for their oil, gas, and precious metals anymore.

John Maynard Keynes believed the government, through banking, interest rate manipulation, and outright decree—remember "fiat" means "by decree"—was the best way to stabilize the economy for all. In a real sense, it was a top down view of how the economy worked. Rather than let the free market work, Keynes wanted to control the value of money and the exchanges it was traded on and what it was traded for.

The period of the early 1970s was the start of a very unsettled time, based on both economic and political strife. In hindsight, it seems obvious that the decision to go off the gold standard was devastating, or at least destabilizing. It didn't lead to the immediate fall of capitalism, but now—more than 30 years later—it has brought us to the precipice, and perhaps the decline, in the dominance of the world economy the United States has enjoyed since the end of World War II. But hindsight is 20/20.

Moreover, inflation and its triggers have opened the door to ideology that is openly opposed to capitalism as a system of progress, innovation, and improvement of the daily lives of people who are not part of the top-down system of governing.

The next period of rapid inflation—today!—will be recognizable and deeply familiar to readers of this book in the early 2020s—a period of runaway inflation comparable only to the period in the 1970s and early 1980s following the dismantling of Bretton Woods. And when the wheels seemed to be coming off from the global economy.

CHAPTER 3

ATTENTION TO DEFICITS DISORDER

Floating currencies lead to the idea that the government can print and spend US dollars indefinitely. Indefinite overspending. Indefinite deficits. Like a college student running around with her parent's credit card at the mall, nations using fiat currencies don't know when to stop. And we know what happens when more and more of something is dumped into a system: the value of each thing gets less.

Enter our favorite government body, the Federal Reserve, or what the author Edward Griffin has famously dubbed "The Creature from Jekyll Island." The institution of a Federal Reserve—a central bank dedicated to controlling the money and the supply of money in the American financial system—began after a financial panic in 1907. But the idea had its genesis years earlier in 1895 when the US Treasury was close to bankruptcy. There was also a financial panic in 1893. By 1895, the great financier JP Morgan struck a deal to sell his own gold reserves to the government for a favorable 30-year bond.

Morgan in effect saved the Treasury but was going "long US economy"—he was helping to save the government, for a tidy profit, so it could remain solvent while his other business ventures played out. Smart. Good work if you can get it.

Well, he got it. In 1907, a dozen years later, there was another banking panic. J.P. Morgan again stepped in with a group of bankers to save the American government. But what could possibly go wrong when a single banker—or even a group of them—control the finances of an entire nation?

There was a theme developing that didn't sit well with the public or many politicians. It also looked like an opportunity for the banking community in New York to build a third central bank.

In November 1910, in a secret meeting at the Jekyll Island Club, off the coast of Georgia, six men—Nelson Aldrich, A. Piatt Andrew, Henry Davison, Arthur Shelton, Frank Vanderlip, and Paul Warburg—met to reform the nation's banking system. What came out of the meeting would, after a few years of intense politicking, create the Federal Reserve, a third central bank for the nation. It also would eventually establish 12 regional Federal Reserve banks—what is known today at the Federal Reserve System.

It's still astounding to economic historians that the Jekyll Island meeting and its intended purpose were kept secret. The six men who met did not even admit the meeting took place for another two decades, long after when their plan had passed through Congress; long after World War I; long after the Roaring '20s and into the Great Depression. Only then was the Jekyll Island meeting revealed.

While the outrage of having a small group of powerful bankers control the nation's finances existed, it was "solved" in a secret meeting by a small group of powerful bankers.

The Federal Reserve Act was ultimately passed in 1913 under the Wilson administration. The act established a bank to preside over the nation's money and the star of our show: the American dollar. And, by extension, the government's ability to issue debt.

TOO BIG TO FAIL?

The shock and awe of the "bailouts"—when the government covers banks' speculative bets by buying bad debt off their hands—initiated by then Secretary of the Treasury, Hank Paulson in 2008 was surprising to monetary historians.

There has been a long series of panics and bailouts in United States monetary history. We could recount the list here. We could name names. We could name conflicts. This treatise would be longer. But our cause here is only to illustrate a more simple point. We've been having the conversation about finance, economics and the markets, the currency and society, since the United States became a nation.

Why do we spend so much time worrying about our recent history? Because it matters to our own wallets. That said, there's good reason to still be anxious: government debt, the historical record of nations in debt, and the management of a fiat currency are not good. Oh yeah, there's that thing about the reserve currency of the world, too, which we will get to later.

If the history of US federal budgets—and the debts that grow out of them—tells us anything, it is this: The dollar is in it up to its eyeballs. Today's level of debt and continuing deficit spending is only the visible portion of that problem; beneath the surface, we face an unavoidable day of reckoning for our great national pastime: spending money.

In reviewing the following history, we make a distinction between deficit spending and the national debt. Many people are confused about the differences, and some, even experts, use debt and deficit interchangeably.

A debt is the total amount of money owed. A deficit is when you don't have enough money to cover your expenses for that fiscal year. Every year that the government runs a deficit adds to the national debt. For example, if the government begins the year with $5 trillion in national debt, and during the year spends $1 trillion more than it brings in in tax revenue, the government is running a deficit of $1 trillion. By the end of the year, that deficit will have increased the national debt to $6 trillion. These are, of course, quaint figures meant to illustrate the point. In 2021, the government deficit was $3.6 trillion bringing the total debt to more than $31 trillion.

Since long before Lord Keynes opened his mouth in the 1930s, the attitude in Washington and among academics has been that we don't really have to ever repay debt. It can be carried indefinitely for future generations to worry about. Most today would claim that debt doesn't matter or even that it is a wise policy to spend more than you bring in. The mind boggles.

Early on in US history, we Americans learned from our British ancestors that empires could be built on a foundation of debt—and continued indefinitely. In the early part of the eighteenth century, Sir Robert Walpole introduced an innovative system for financing Britain's colonial expansion and ever-growing military might. Government, Walpole demonstrated, is able to create a revenue stream by issuing bonds and other debt instruments. The interest is paid regularly, and eventually, upon maturity, the face value is paid off—and for every maturing bond, a new one is issued. This simple method for the expansion of revenue through debt was the venue by which Britain built its empire, from the 1720s through the next 100 years. Among those who observed this phenomenon of endless debt financing was the first secretary of the Treasury of the United States, Alexander Hamilton.

In the early days of the American nation, a host of fiscal problems faced Hamilton and the other Founding Fathers. The War for Independence left a large debt; there was no unified currency, and each state issued its own money; the currency itself was of dubious value; and inflation made it difficult to imagine how the young nation would even survive. Hamilton's view was that growth and expansion would be possible with the use of debt:

> Hamilton's rationale for a perpetual public debt included his belief that it would help keep up taxes and preserve the collection apparatus. He believed Americans inclined toward laziness and needed to be taxed to prod them to work harder.[1]

Not everyone agreed. In Thomas Jefferson's view,

> It was unjust and unrepublican for one generation of a nation to encumber the next with the obligation to discharge the debts of the first. After all, the following generation cannot have given their consent to decisions made by their fathers, nor will they have necessarily benefited from the deficit expenditures.[2]

> During the nineteenth century, American debt did not grow substantially. When Jefferson began his first presidential term in 1801, the nation had an $83 million debt, mostly left over from the costs of the war. During his two terms, Jefferson reduced the debt to $37 million even after spending $15 million on the Louisiana Purchase. The early stewards of the nation's money were at least conscientious of the value it brought to citizens.

It wasn't until 1965 that politicians started spending on political promises so aggressively, that the value of the dollar—the amount of goods and services you could buy with each one—took a precipitous turn. The demise accelerated in 1971.

$37 in 1809, adjusted for inflation

Using the official CPI data calculator,[3] it's easy to see what happened to the value of the dollar in the presence of political values. What it took to earn a living and raise a family, run a farm, maybe send kids to school, was relatively stable for a little more than 150 years. Then politicians learned they could promise the national bounty in exchange for votes. It's not Washington or Wall Street who get strongarmed by the demise of the dollar; it's everyday Americans who are trying to make ends meet.

Buying power of $37 over time, 1809–2022

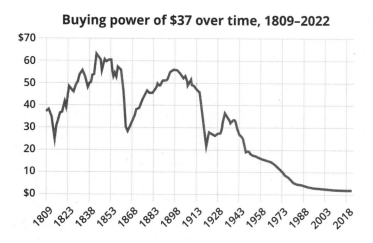

For a couple periods in the ensuing history, most notably in 1838 and 1898, then again briefly in 1929, the purchasing power of the dollar rose. Since Bretton Woods in 1944 and the end of World War II, the US dollar hasn't been able to buy as much as it did the year before.

BACK TO THE FUTURE

In James Madison's term of office, the ill-fated War of 1812 ran the national debt up to $127 million by 1816. James Monroe and John Quincy Adams were both able to reduce the debt during their terms of office, and by 1829 the debt had fallen to $58 million. And then, during Andrew Jackson's presidency, the national debt was entirely paid off. For the first and only time in its history (and the last) the United States had no national debt.

Unfortunately, the attention to deficits disorder began soon after. And never went away. It's a progressive condition, meaning once it starts, it's hard to stop. By the modern era in which we're writing, it has become a full blown psychosis. During the early part of the country's history, presidents and Congress saw it as their duty to either balance the books or at least pay off debt incurred for defense or expansion of the national boundaries. (Where are these people today, one wants to ask in the most cynical way possible?)

Over the decade following Madison, the country ran up $46 million in new debt, and by 1848 the national debt had risen to $63 million. However, in all fairness, one advantage of this was that the Mexican War resulted in US expansion all the way to the Pacific and the acquisition of the entire Southwest, including California. Under the Franklin Pierce administration, the debt was paid down to $28 million, but it never got that low again.

The Civil War exploded the national debt up to $2.8 *billion,* or 100 times higher than it had been in 1857. Debt in 1860 was $2 per capita; at the end of 1865, per capita debt was $75. The temporary tax measures in place during the war were repealed, and by the end of the nineteenth century the debt had been reduced to $1.2 billion, less than half of its 1865 level.[4]

Given the vast expansion of US territory and the wars the country fought to create and then hold together the United States, this does not seem a large debt level. In fact, in its first 110 years of history, the United States had shown its ability to fund expansion while reducing debt over time. And this was accomplished without an income tax. In fact, in 1869 and again in 1895, the Supreme Court ruled federal income taxes unconstitutional.

The story was quite different in the twentieth century. By the end of World War I, the national debt had risen to $26 billion. Even though the debt level had been reduced over the next decade, the Great Depression caused further deficit spending, and FDR's New Deal tripled debt levels up to $72 billion.

World War II created yet higher debt levels. By 1945, the country owed $260 billion—small by today's standards but gargantuan in its time. One outgrowth of that war was a new one, the Cold War. Military spending took the national debt up to $930 billion by 1980, and under Ronald Reagan's administration it rose to nearly $2.7 trillion. Ten years later, after Bill Clinton's eight years, the debt more than doubled to $5.6 trillion. In other words, the national debt was already growing exponentially.

There are always political justifications. For Reagan it was the Cold War. Clinton rearranged some numbers, and it looked like the United States was on its way to a decline in the rate at which the debt was increasing. Then came 9/11 and the War on Terror. Globalization and a new competitive international market gave its incentive. All the while, the levels of debt kept setting new records, virtually on a month-to-month basis. In 2005, the US debt was already growing at a rate of $1.4 billion a day on the first edition of this book, more than $1 million a minute; "the most famous debt clock in the country," we wrote at the time, "located on Times Square in New York City, will become obsolete once it hits the $10 trillion mark."

Ten trillion dollars now seems like a quaint figure.[5]

Our political class's incapacity to pay attention to deficits has propelled us beyond $31 trillion as of December 2022. Of course, we had the pandemic to help justify this latest acceleration in spending and debt accumulation.

I still love the following comments, issued in a joint October 2007 statement by Henry Paulson, the secretary of the US Treasury, and Jim Nussle, the director of the administration's Office of Management

US National Debt, 1789–2022
Source: pgpf.org

Source: Peter G. Peterson Foundation

and Budget. Paulson: "This year's budget results demonstrate the remarkable strength of the US economy. This strength has translated into record-breaking revenues flowing into the US Treasury and a continued decline in the federal budget deficit."

True, but we still have annual deficits. Even more massive ones now. And the ensuing, prevailing, mindset from 2008 through 2020 (the pandemic year) didn't change anything. Debt has become institutionalized. While citizens may be concerned, government—including both the elected representatives and those who remain year after year in the growing bureaucracy—are inoculated to annual deficits and the skyrocketing national debt.

In 2007, Nussle continued back: "Our short-term budget outlook is improving, but beyond the horizon is a huge budgetary challenge—the unsustainable growth in Social Security, Medicare, and Medicaid; . . . for the sake of our children and grandchildren, Congress should begin to take action to prevent this fiscal train wreck." They did the opposite. For years. Who gets held accountable? Virtually and realistically, no one.

DEBT AND SPENDING ABOVE OUR MEANS

Why does the government need to spend more than it takes in? After all, in most of the nineteenth century there were no income taxes, except during the Civil War. And the debts the nation incurred were paid down time and again. Even by 1900 the debt level was manageable. Not so today. Not even close.

So what are the root causes of deficit spending and the resulting debt?

In short, debt itself has become institutionalized. Today, many people simply accept as a fact of life that the national debt is unimaginably high. There aren't too many people alive who have lived in a time when it wasn't.

The problem, though, is that we cannot continue the exponential expansion of debt without a catastrophic economic outcome. And it isn't just the stated trillions of dollars of official debt. If you add in the obligations of the US government under Medicare and Social Security, the real overall debt is many times higher than the 2007 level of more than $9 trillion. The real debt in 2007 was estimated at almost six times higher, about $53 trillion.[6] Other estimates are that such "mandatory spending programs . . . actually inflate the national debt by a factor of 10."[7]

"How much is $53 trillion?" we asked 15 years ago. "It is difficult to imagine," we tried to answer. "A stack of $100 bills would be about five feet high to reach $1 million. A $1 billion stack would be one mile high, and a $1 trillion stack would be 1,000 miles high. So $53 trillion would equal 53,000 miles of tightly stacked $100 bills, which would reach around the earth more than twice!"

That was astounding when we wrote it the first time. Fast forward to December 2022, the unfunded liabilities of the US government are now estimated to be nearly $148 trillion—nearly three times as much. So using basic math, we could now circle the earth six times with a mammoth, gargantuan, ridiculously large stack of $100 bills.

And that is one huge problem with explaining the severity of US debt levels is that the real scope of the problem is beyond imagination. And since we mostly use digits on computers now, rather than paper bills, the analogy is practically moot. We're beyond imagining what a real hole we've dug ourselves into.

The situation we have seen growing throughout the twentieth century, since the founding of the Federal Reserve, is going to come home to roost in our future. Historically, it's just a fact. Policy makers and career politicians seem to actually believe they can beat 5,000 years of human history.

A FAIRY-TALE ECONOMY

During the Clinton administration, when the government boasted of "budget surpluses," there really was no surplus at all. Even if we confine the discussion to the stated debt, we realize that in the eight years from 1992 to 2000, the debt rose from $4.065 trillion to $5.674 trillion. The claimed surpluses, or what one scholar has called a "surplus hoax," were achieved through a little trickery:

> Imagine a corporation suffering losses and being deep in debt. In order to boost its stock prices and the bonuses of its officers, the corporation quietly borrows funds in the bond market and uses them not only to cover its losses but also to retire some corporate stock and thereby bid up its price. And imagine the management boasting of profits and surpluses. But that's what the Clinton administration has been doing with alacrity and brazenness. It suffers sizable budget deficits, increasing the national debt by hundreds of billions of dollars, but uses trust funds to meet expenditures and then boasts of surpluses, which excites the spending predilection of politicians in both parties.[8]

> In the Clinton years, the administration churned obligations through short-term debt in the hope that interest rates would not increase. At the same time, the Congressional Budget Office estimated that federal spending for Social Security and Medicare would grow from 7.5% of gross domestic product (GDP) in 1999 up to 16.7% by 2040.[9] So the claim of budget surpluses was disingenuous not only insofar as it described the nominal national debt but also because it ignored the reality of ever-larger long-term obligations under government programs.

Clinton-era Treasury Secretary Robert Rubin's scheme was continued in a sense by Treasury head Paul O'Neill in the administration of George W. Bush. (This fiscal philosophy came to be known sarcastically as "Rubinomics.") By 2002, it was clear that neither party had any serious intention of respecting a debt ceiling. Although such a ceiling exists, it is constantly revised by Congress as the debt continues its upward acceleration unchecked. In fact, since 1960 the debt ceiling has been raised 78 times. One wonders why they bother calling it a "ceiling" at all.[10]

The post-9/11 imperative to fight the War on Terror—coupled with a stated desire to jump-start the economy—led President Bush to present ever-higher budgets while insisting on tax cuts. Were these initiatives accompanied by a serious reduction in government itself, it would make sense; otherwise, we are left with ever-higher budgets in which spending is invariably higher than revenues. It has become clear that both parties and the entire federal government reside in their own economic cloud-cuckoo-land.[11]

Ironically, the Federal Reserve's attempts to stimulate the economy via ever-lower interest rates led to a huge expansion in credit, both among consumers and in government. So we ended up with a mortgage bubble in addition to the other economic bubbles brought about by debt-based economic expansion. As housing prices grew nationally by 5% to 7% per year, consumers continually refinanced to remove equity at lower and lower rates, further fueling the bubble.

The official position concerning economic expansion ignored the reality. Then-Fed Chairman Alan Greenspan repeatedly pointed to high levels of consumer spending as evidence of a strong economy. This ignored the basic economic principle that makes a distinction between productive and consumptive debt. An example of productive debt is investment in plant and machinery, which leads to higher and more competitive manufacturing—a type of activity that is falling in the United States, not rising.

Economists recognize that productive debt leads to permanent and long-term economic growth. In contrast, consumptive debt—which is the modern basis for the economic "recovery" pointed to often by the Fed and the Bush administration—is spending to purchase material goods. The spending does not go into savings or investment; it merely involves buying more stuff. And the modern form of consumptive debt is based on growing levels of credit card and mortgage debt. The consumer-based credit problem mirrors the national debt (and longer-term national obligation) problem. It is growing.

In the past, conservative politicians stood for balanced budgets and fiscal responsibility—or at least that was the claim. But beginning with the Reagan years, the concept of lower taxes as a generator of higher revenues, what Bush senior once termed "voodoo economics," became the new rule. Reagan ran on the promise of smaller government, spending cuts, and balanced budgets. But in Reagan's very first year in office, in 1981, he asked Congress to increase the statutory debt limit above $1 trillion. Argued for as a one-time measure needed to bring the economic house into line, this departure opened up a new era; and now, a quarter century later, we find ourselves at nine times the $1 trillion "magic number" of the pre-Reagan debt ceiling. The inane argument offered up by Professor Abba Lerner in the 1930s, and also repeated in many other economic textbooks, is that there is nothing wrong with a national debt because "we owe it to ourselves"[12] demonstrates the twisted thinking used to justify current policies. It is the same thing as saying it is all right as consumers to pile on mortgage debt on our homes because "we owe it to ourselves" in the sense that it is our equity. Astute homeowners would not accept such a vacuous argument, and yet it is offered with a straight face by some economists concerning the national debt.

Another justification is often put forth that the US "net worth" justifies ever-higher debt levels. In other words, as long as our assets are higher than our liabilities, a large national debt is no problem.

Vast land holdings via national parks and preserves, government buildings, and other valuable assets, for example, are cited as examples that we have nothing to worry about. We get that there is a bounty in the land. But under current administrative law that bounty is owned by the government and subject to political will.

The argument fails on the merits. On corporate balance sheets, one justification for growing debt would be that it enables the expansion of markets and capital assets. But let us not forget that the federal government produces nothing. The debt may go partially for necessities or entitlements that large segments of the population want to continue, but the debt itself is not an example of productive debt. So the arguments that it's okay because (1) we owe it to ourselves or (2) our assets are greater than our liabilities are both false justifications for a problem that, ultimately, may define the collapse of the entire US economy. Who's ready for that?

In fact, we don't "owe it to ourselves." The phrase itself became popular in the mid-2000s when public debt was still being debated in public. "We owe it to ourselves" implies that the United States economy exists independent of the globally connected economy we all depend on. Alas, Congress doesn't even debate public debt anymore, except when the debt ceiling debate comes up and the parties have to shirk and say something like, "Yeah, but if we don't agree the government will be shut down," and their gravy trains will also shrivel up and become inedible.

The real fact is, the portion of the national debt held by foreign central banks grows month after month, and in the near future a majority of the stated debt will be held overseas. And let me repeat again what is becoming the mantra of this third edition: the more you run up in the system, the less each individual dollar is worth.

It was true when we wrote the first edition of *Demise of the Dollar*, it's even more true now. At the end of 2006, the amount of our debt held by foreigners had increased by $463.9 billion during the year, to $2.7 trillion. That's 46% of the national debt at the time—up from 44% in 2005. Two percentage points in a year was a very big deal then. By 2021, just the top three countries holding US debt—Japan, China, and the United Kingdom—totaled more than $2.8 trillion. The next 10 countries on the list from Luxembourg to India account for another $2.8 trillion. That brings the total among the top 13 holders of US debt to $5.6 trillion.[13] (This will be an important point to keep in mind when we discuss the dollar's role as the "reserve currency" of the global economy.)

Economists enjoy comparing government debt to entrepreneurial debt. In 2008, we observed "the highly leveraged business owner Donald Trump has suffered financial reversals and even the bankruptcy of his casino empire; but at least he provides jobs, construction activity, and commerce for thousands of people. His debt, while leveraged, is an example of productive debt."

GOOD DEBT VERSUS BAD DEBT

In spite of the long-standing belief that people in debt are habitually poor and creditors are habitually rich, it's often the other way around. In fact, in business the more successful entrepreneurs are often also the most in debt (but productive debt). This has no comparison to government debt, which—again, it may be classified as necessary or even contractual with the people receiving entitlements—is not a form of productive debt. As long as Congress has the attitude that higher revenues (even if artificial) open the door to higher spending levels, this economic promiscuity is not likely to end, at least not until the end is imposed upon Congress, and upon the people.

Government spending is not productive for two reasons. As explained earlier, the government produces nothing in the form of investment or capital assets. But in addition, it generates no revenues. It finances its own growth and expansion in three ways. First is tax revenue, or taking of money from people, corporations, and imports. Second is inflation, a system under which debt literally loses value and can be repaid with depreciated dollars. Third is debt itself, an expansion of the system that has no end until an end is imposed upon the government. The trouble with the third item is the government must impose the limits on itself. You may be aware that every few years Congress has to vote to increase the "debt ceiling" or it will run out of funding for its own operations. They make a big deal out of it on the floor of the House of Representatives and in the media, but invariably both parties want to increase the debt ceiling and vote to do so.

In the nineteenth century, a series of presidents took debt seriously and, other than in periods of war, diligently paid down the national debt. It may be coincidental, but that all changed at about the same time that the federal income tax was imposed. After repeated decisions by the US Supreme Court that the federal tax was unconstitutional, the Court finally accepted the tax in 1913. Since then, deficit spending has become the rule and balanced budgets the exception. The concept of actually paying down the debt is an oddity. The even more distant idea of eliminating the federal debt is viewed as unrealistic, even un-American. But we should recall the warning provided 250 years ago by Adam Smith:

> It is the highest impertinence and presumption . . . in kings and ministers to pretend to watch over the economy of private people, and to restrain their expense.[14]

The chosen path of the United States, in spite of Smith's wise warning, was to come to view the national debt as a "national blessing."[15] Well, an unbridled spending program may indeed be viewed as

Debt rises and falls with wars and changes in the economy.
Debt is currently at its highest level since 1946

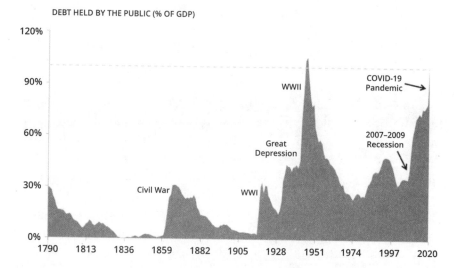

DEBT HELD BY THE PUBLIC (% OF GDP)

Source: https://www.itsuptous.org/US-National-Debt?gclid=CjwKCAiAs8acBhA1EiwAgRFdw1hlNyytMk4Axu9 hpaCrONUaUb3g9MGQnRxbYNKxBVlf2JRvCleq8hoCZh0QAvD_BwE#US_National_Debt_Over_Time

a national blessing by those in Congress and among economists who justify debt levels by classifying the debt as productive debt. But any honest study of how and where government spending occurs would have to conclude that the undisciplined growth of the debt is anything but productive.

While the national debt ebbs and grows with wars and pandemics, it's currently at its highest percentage of GDP since 1946, just after World War II. They call this the debt-to-GDP ratio. But in our current political environment, there's little appetite, or resources, for paying it down as was done following the war. Loads of people in government believe, perhaps sincerely, that deficit spending is a positive force, that it works to improve the economy. As we've shown, it's been going on for generations. The idea is taught in colleges and universities. Students leave believing there are no lasting negative consequences. And why should they?

Congress appears either to agree with this point of view, or to go along with it, in the interest of spending ever higher levels of public money. It's public money. Which means it has to be raised from taxes. Even though often expressed as a joke, we should view Congress in light of this now famous congressman's comment,

> I've had a tough time learning how to act like a congressman. Today I accidentally spent some of my own money.[16]

One of the most destructive facts—and one obstructing any reform of the problem—is that those in Congress do not think about public money as real money. There exists an intentional self-imposed disconnect between what Congress spends and who pays for it.

Because the House of Representatives create the spending initiatives, there is no will among those elected to change the rules.

Complicating the dialogue is the never-ending class warfare surrounding government spending and tax policy itself. Republicans claim that tax cuts stimulate growth and improve the jobs situation, thus improving the economy overall. Democrats criticize the "huge tax cuts for the rich" as a burden on less fortunate Americans. Both arguments are flawed in some degree, but the appeal is made to distinct voting blocs. Class warfare based on envy and resentment does nothing to improve the understanding of the problem among the people; in fact, arguments made with a political bias only close the door to any meaningful education or discussion of the problem—ever-higher debt (of both the public and the government), trade deficits, and numerous economic bubbles.

In the final analysis, it does not matter whether we raise or lower taxes if spending outpaces revenue. Higher taxes affect consumers, creators, business owners, and investors. Higher government spending that consistently outpaces its own tax revenues does greater damage in the long term. Anyone with common sense can see the system is unsustainable. No one is saying the folks who are making these decisions are stupid or unable to understand. The perversion of their own self-interest is what's at stake. To survive politically, they must comply. I believe, if you asked any member of the House or Senate if they agree with the way allocations of public funds are distributed they'd say, "No, I don't agree." And yet, each spending bill makes its way through. Tit for tat. My plan, for yours. The cost goes up. And then it goes up again. And again.

Here's the problem: The Representatives and Senators don't pay for any bills they propose. You and I do.

And yet, somehow, especially since Donald Trump entered the political fray, we think the system of lobbying and influence in Washington can be fixed. We think the "revolving door" between Wall Street and Washington will, what, suddenly not happen in the next administration, the next generation? Influence is what it is. Mind you, I have written on several occasions, the worst thing Donald Trump did in his career was get into politics; he made people care about politics again.

The result is clear. The value of the dollar is undermined when the government spends beyond its means. While these differences may be obvious to many, one Congressional report did a good job of comparing the two, in respect not only to their attributes but also to the economic consequences and ramifications involved. Pointing out that an individual is able to offset deficits by working harder, spending less, or applying for a temporary loan, the report notes:

> In contrast, government revenue comes mainly from taxes, which are compulsory. When government increases its revenue by increasing its tax collections, there is no presumption that people will be better off.

> They may not want to give more of their income to the government. Therefore, closing a budget deficit by raising more revenue does not necessarily make the economy grow; it can discourage growth by making leisure time and other untaxed activity relatively more attractive. Raising tax rates, or keeping them higher than they need be, increases what economists call the "deadweight loss" or "excess burden" of taxation—income that is not transferred from taxpayers to government, but is simply lost because excessive taxation reduces economic growth by inducing people to behave less productively.[17]

This observation is true, but it refers to only part of the problem. History has demonstrated that tax policy does not help eliminate deficits. Increased taxes have not closed budget deficits, but have only inspired Congress to spend more; and reductions in the tax rate have one of two outcomes, depending on which side you believe: Either these lower taxes only add to the deficit, or the resulting "trickle-down" revenues—again—result in higher annual budgets and the resulting higher deficits.

What if we didn't think of the Federal Reserve and the government as the beginning and the end of economic activity? That might change things a little. Alas!

A recurring argument in all of this debate over taxes and the national debt is that deficit spending actually helps the economy through stimulus. We saw this in spades with the direct stimulus checks to individuals or households during the government-mandated lockdowns beginning in March 2020. In fact, the government has come to view its role in the economy as a driving force that can and should take steps to fix recessions or to curb inflation. In times of recession, the proposal to increase government spending is invariably argued as a method for fixing the problem.[18]

What do we say now of post-pandemic lockdowns? Of inflation after increasing the money supply? After a decade of interest rates at zero or in some cases negative levels? What about Fed policy when it declares it has to slay inflation. . .that it caused? What are we to make of their press conferences and the Fed minutes that get released?

The argument defies logic. Especially in a free society. Governments produce nothing. Governments doesn't make anything. They don't make goods or move them on rail lines or produce energy. They don't grow food or make cool sports shoes. They don't grow or distribute coffee. You get the point. There is no logical way that increased spending for government services would have any positive effect on the economy.

The one thing the government has, by law, is the power to enforce contracts. It has a role in protecting its citizens, from threats internal and external. Government has a role in helping to encourage and supporting economic exchange among a free people. Today, however, government is used as a tool to regulate and prohibit the economy from flourishing based on the special interests of those who pull the strings. Our political process is not so much a debate on who gets to run the government efficiently, but rather who gets to divide the spoils.

Were the argument made to increase investment in manufacturing plants and equipment, provide incentives to higher savings, or actually reduce government deficit spending, it might make sense. But claiming that higher spending on the part of government would fix an economic recession is like claiming that the best way to put out a fire is to pour gasoline on a burning house.

There are situations in which deficit spending has a positive impact on the economy, but such instances are limited, to say the least. When such spending reallocates resources from less productive use and into more productive use, it is conceivable that deficit spending would improve a weak economy. But as a general observation, government spending has the opposite effect, reallocating resources from more productive use and into *less* productive use.[19]

The problem with using taxing policy in an attempt to control the economy has historically been ineffective. This may be true in part because tax policy has so often been used to reward or punish, to feed into the class warfare and resentment we see in different voting groups. Tax policy has done more to widen the gap between classes than any other force in US history. The problem goes beyond the arrogance to believe that the economy can be tinkered with, as though a simple adjustment of the tax thermostat is all it takes to fix the problem.

Tax policy is far more complex, and the consequences of changes in policy invariably belie even the best of intentions. This inevitability was explained more than 150 years ago by Senator John C. Calhoun, who stated:

> On all articles on which duties can be imposed, there is a point in the rate of duties which may be called the maximum point of revenue—that is, a point at which the greatest amount of revenue would be raised. If it be elevated above that, the importation of the article would fall off more rapidly than the duty would be raised; and, if depressed below it, the reverse effect would follow: that is, the duty would decrease more rapidly than the importation would increase.[20]

Although Calhoun was arguing about a tariff bill, the same point applies to the income taxes; the difficulty is in identifying the "maximum point of revenue." That varies depending on the political party in power, the desired voting bloc to which the speaker is appealing, and the economic perception in play. It appears evident that the point resides somewhere around a 20% effective tax rate. Above that level, individual behavior erodes economic performance and, thus, revenues.[21]

The point is, the government can't control the economy through tax policy or any other policy—a lesson the government, a body of representatives with contrary incentives, has yet to learn. And frankly may never learn. Most, in my opinion, care more about getting re-elected than representing their constituents. The incentives are completely misaligned. It's an age old conundrum, but worth understanding.

The recent economic history of the United States has been based on the premise that government initiatives can (and should) affect and even alter the course of the economy. Looking back, we see a clear distinction between the eras in US history. From 1789 through 1912, government appeared to understand that the economy operated independently from government. In fact, as national debts were accumulated (as during the Revolutionary War, the War of 1812, and the Civil War), subsequent administrations paid those debts down. The presidents during those first 125 years or so took their responsibilities seriously and recognized the real nature of the national debt.

Government does hold the power to finance its various programs, and even wars, through building up national debt. But that debt—at least during the first 125 years of US history—was *not* viewed as a permanent fixture in the US economy. Rather, the view appears to have been that debts accumulated in one period must be reduced or paid off in another.

From 1913 forward, we entered a different phase. Beginning with the three major changes that occurred that year (passage of Owen-Glass Act, which created the Federal Reserve System; the Seventh Amendment, which eliminated state legislature election of senators;[22] and creation of the federal income tax), the whole view toward the economy and the government's role changed once and for all. Monetary policy was no longer viewed as an adjunct of government's economic role; it became a primary tool in the control over the pace and direction of the economy itself. Government became the economic god in the twentieth century, and monetary and tax policy was available to reward allies and to punish enemies. To me, that's contrary to a well-run republic.

With this new direction—used quite specifically by Presidents Wilson, Roosevelt, Nixon, and Clinton, for example—the line between economic policy and political incentive grew ever less distinct. Today, we see no line whatsoever. Economic and monetary policies are debated along party lines for the most part, with both sides pushed further apart as the political debate heats up and as the next election cycle approaches.

The fallout from this nearly 100 years of monetary adventurism has no end in sight. We've lived with an income tax for nearly 100 years, but our national debt is higher than ever; in fact, it is higher than anyone could have imagined in 1913. Is there a connection? Clearly, there is. The nature of government is to spend more than it receives, and as the income tax has become an institution in the United States, government spending has consistently outpaced revenues. Prior to 1913, debts came and went, but importantly, they went. Presidents and Congress did not overspend because the revenues simply were not available, so the lack of an income tax made it impossible to accelerate the debt problem.

Today, when the gold standard is but a distant memory, it has become possible for the United States and the Federal Reserve to authorize reduced interest rates and increased deficit spending.

If we look back to the decisions made during the Nixon administration, two forces were at work. First was inflation, a chronic problem Nixon tried to fix with wage and price controls and import tariffs. Second was the overprinting of money that led to the risk of a run on gold—the so-called international margin call. Nixon's solution was simply to remove the United States from the gold standard and allow unending printing of money.

It is the printing of unpegged fiat money that led to yet more inflation. In more recent years, government and the Federal Reserve have figured out how to make it look as though no inflation is taking place. Low interest rates equal no inflation, right? According to the Federal Reserve, low rates are good for the economy. But by definition, inflation means a loss of spending power. That can be viewed as one of two outcomes: higher prices or less purchasing power for our dollars.

As we measure inflation, it is elusive. The consumer price index (CPI) includes many components—food, durable goods, housing, fuel, and more. Often, as one price sector rises, another falls. On balance, we have a published rate of inflation that is supposed to explain how our dollar buys more or less. A shortfall between wages and prices means a loss of spending power, under traditional definitions. But if we measure the dollar against the euro, we get a more realistic view of inflation. In fact, as more and more fiat money is printed, we continue to lose spending power, which is most accurately measured against other currencies.

Among the changes that followed Nixon's 1971 decision was a change in the way that government debt was financed. Deficit finance bonds are sold through the financial markets to private investors. Of course, "private investors" does not limit the market to mutual funds or individuals in the United States; overseas central banks are included as well. The bond market exploded as a result of this change. In 1970, less than $1 trillion in bonds were issued. By 2006, the volume grew to $45 trillion.[23]

The change has, effectively, made price inflation invisible in the US landscape. Author Peter Warburton has summarized this problem:

> Periodic bouts of price inflation, the tell-tale signs of a long-standing debt addiction, have all but vanished. The central banks, as financial physicians, seem to have effected a cure. . . . Few have bothered to ask how the central banks have accomplished this feat, one which has proven elusive for more than 20 years. As long as inflation is absent, who really cares exactly what the central banks have been up to?[24]

It is naive to believe—or to act upon the assumption—that prices of goods will naturally or automatically change based on the supply of money in circulation. (In other words, today's goods cost $1 to produce and sell for $2 retail; so if currency in circulation increases, costs rise to $2 and the retail price goes up to $4.) In fact, this is not how inflation works. Even so, it would seem that the US government and the Federal Reserve believe this to be the case. A weak dollar diminishes the economic impact of the national debt and trade surplus, so that is a good thing, is it not?

Even if we were to accept the flawed premise dictating that changes in the money supply can, by association, affect prices, it makes no sense that this presumption also makes it acceptable to grow trade deficits and the national debt to higher and higher levels. The belief requires us to accept another premise: that we can solve all economic problems and shortfalls by continuing to print more and more money.

Many economists have had the uncomfortable suspicion for some time now that the US government is playing the game of interest rate arbitrage, a practice begun under the Clinton administration and a cornerstone of Rubinomics. This "carry trade" involves selling low-yielding, short-term Treasury bills and using the money to buy much higher-yielding, longer-term notes and bonds. In other words, the concept involves using US debt to profit from the differences between the debt tiers. Even if this worked, it would not justify the endless printing of more currency.

So the two practices—operating on the assumption that currency in circulation controls prices, and promoting interest rate arbitrage—are part of US economic policy. The Achilles' heel of such a plan (even if we accept the underlying premises of each side) is that as long as the United States continues to accumulate annual deficits (as well as trade surpluses and other economic bubbles), the US dollar will continue to weaken. This real inflation may not have an immediate impact on consumer prices across the board, but its ramifications are certainly felt in both equity and debt investment markets. Lower yields reflect not only historically low interest rates, but a growing recognition in the markets that the dollar's purchasing power is falling. In a very real sense, a decline in investment values reflects the inflationary spiral. Our modern variety of inflation is seen not in prices and wages directly as in the Nixon years, but in stock and bond prices.

During the ill-fated 1972 campaign of George McGovern—double-digit points behind Nixon in the weeks before election day—the candidate made an attempt to swing the mood in his favor. He promised $1,000 to every American man, woman, and child. But failing to articulate how he would pay for this, how much it would cost, or what it was meant to accomplish, the idea only increased Nixon's lead. Voters instinctively recognized that the proposal was a lame one. Were we to increase everyone's bank account by $1,000, we would inevitably see inflation as an offset, either in higher prices or in reduced purchasing power of the dollar. The electorate didn't buy McGovern's plan then, but, ironically, a similar approach to the economy permeates government and Federal Reserve policy today. The unlimited printing of fiat money enabled us to think that we would expand and grow forever, in a credit and debt bubble without end.

"Household net worth may not continue to rise relative to income," Alan Greenspan admitted on a book tour early in 2005, "and some reversal in that ratio is not out of the question. If that were to occur, households would probably perceive the need to save more out of current income; the personal savings rate would accordingly rise, and consumer spending would slow."[25]

Was he ever wrong. The exact opposite happened: Personal savings fell below zero, while consumer spending increased. The impact took the air out of the subprime mortgage and credit bubbles.

In the third quarter of 2007, the Mortgage Bankers Association reported that the number of Americans who fell behind on their mortgage payments rose to a 20-year high. An incredible 5.59% of all home loans in the United States were at least 30 days late on one or more monthly payments—the worst delinquency rate since 1986— and one in every five subprime adjustable-rate mortgages suffered a late payment.

Does the Fed have a solution? Sure—but it's only for a chosen few: about 145,000 to 240,000 borrowers who began facing rate resets beginning in the third quarter of 2007. Bernanke estimated that 450,000 borrowers will face the music every month, so we're talking 2.3 million by the end of 2008. Meanwhile, the ratings agencies keep lowering the boom on the mortgage-backed assets or securities that funded these mortgages. The count is now somewhere in the neighborhood of a thousand bonds and securities that have been downgraded—and we're not done yet.

Like Greenspan, Bernanke also bemoans the possibility of slower production and profits among American companies as though that trend were separate from the Fed's monetary policies. In November 2007, the Institute for Supply Management (ISM) reported that US manufacturing grew at its slowest pace in 10 months, 50.8 (once that measure falls to 50, ISM considers the sector to be in "contraction"). The service sector—where ISM considers 80% of the economy to lie, by the way—didn't do well, either: The index fell to 54.1 from October's 55.8, making November the worst month since March. (Until, that is, January of 2008, when it fell to 41.) In fact, a corporate trend toward soft or falling profits accompanied a business trend—starting in the 1980s—away from investment in tangible assets and more toward speculation. We know now that much of the reportedly spectacular corporate growth of the 1990s was the result not of profitable growth, but of accounting manipulation.

DEBT ON STEROIDS

The ill-conceived concept that executive compensation should be based on reported profits only invited the kind of abuses everyone saw in corporations like Enron and Tyco, and even among accounting firms like Arthur Andersen. They also opened the door to strange episodes of fraud like the FTX crypto exchange, which declared bankruptcy on November 11, 2022, after having achieved a market cap of $35 billion. Do these episodes simply elicit the mood, both corporate and economic? Or was the phony growth created out of pure greed? In the case of the FTX, there was little corporate governance. And they were colluding with another firm also founded by the CEO Sam Bankman-Fried to trade in FTX's own crypto currency, FTT.[26]

These are troubling questions. Without any doubt, the corporate deceptions that took place throughout the 1990s, during the mortgage-backed securities scam that brought down Lehman Brothers in 2008 and the cryptocurrency crisis in 2022, all created a "phony recovery" that only papers over the truth. Of course, a lot of greed was involved. But on a larger scale, this corporate deception went hand in hand with the Fed policies Greenspan, Bernanke, and Yellen promoted throughout their tenures at the helm of the Federal Reserve. The 1990s asset bubble had a huge impact on the economy of the time, and consumers paid the price. We did not have a strong economy during that period, but government and corporate America went to great pains to make it look as though we did. That trend continued through the tech bubble in the early 2000s, through the bailout period that followed the financial panic of 2008, and all the way up to the lockdowns of the pandemic.

To appreciate the impact of this fake economic strength, we have to consider four distinct features: changes in the trend moving away from investment and toward consumption, profitability, the trade balance, and growth of debt.

One day we hear about consumer debt, and on another we're told that savings rates are falling. But most people don't know how this affects them *or* the purchasing power of their dollar. With ever-expanding consumption, savings rates are down below zero of disposable income. And for all the money Americans accumulate on credit cards and higher mortgage debt, the federal government budget deficit is expanding at an even greater rate.

The warnings given out in the 1990s pale in comparison to the bigger bubbles we face now. A large portion of newly created credit flows into the financial markets, you know, *lenders* who, through mortgages, credit cards, and lines of credit—all those solicitations you get in the mail—collect interest on this rising consumer debt. On one side, as the debt rises, so do the revenues from interest within those financial markets. On the other, when debts default, revenues evaporate, as we saw from massive write-downs being taken by banks in the wake of the subprime mortgage mess and we're seeing again in the wake of the historic inflation of the 2020s.

Our basic economics instructor would remind us that recovery requires business confidence in the economy and that confidence takes the form of investment in plant, equipment, and inventory. This is the key to increasing American standards of living and to sustained productivity (translation: higher-wage jobs, competitive industry, reduction of the trade deficit).

How do we move from today's poor economic situation characterized by a pillaged business infrastructure and return to the days of American dominance over world manufacturing? American corporations do not generally accumulate productive capital today; they, like the consumer, acquire debt to hold their ratios steady. Look at Motorola, for example. This company was a leader in affordable electronics for many years, before market share began to slip and move overseas. The solution? Motorola increased its long-term debt. This enabled the company to keep a strong working capital ratio (because current cash balances rose as long-term debt obligations were taken on), meaning that *current* assets and liabilities maintained the equilibrium of more profitable days. But in fact, the stockholders are stuck with long-term obligations to pay interest on those debt levels, in an environment where the company's revenues and profits are falling. In spite of what our Fed chairman says, increasing debt is *not* productivity. It is a disastrous policy.

If corporations depend too heavily on debt capitalization at the expense of equity, it eventually spells doom for them. The Fed is more aggressive than this lesson in basic economics. "Pushing on a string" the old timers called it. Meaning, you can get away with your strategy until the string breaks.

What the Fed has termed "wealth creation"—from Greenspan, Bernanke and Yellen through Jerome Powell—is nothing more than that infamous series of bubbles. Granted, Jay Powell has been putting on a grim face. But clearly, growth in housing values leading to refinancing, higher transactions, and inflation in housing values did not lead to wealth creation; it was credit expansion. If we spend more in consumption than in production, we do not get richer; we give more money to bankers. The same is true for a nation in our global position and trade relationships.

Rising stock values or housing values add to equity and immediate net worth. The opposite is also true. As an individual, if your home doubles in value, then your capital appears to be worth twice as much. The wealth creation is real in a sense because you invested money in real estate. If the same profitability occurred in the stock market, it would be because you invested money in stocks. If either real estate or stocks decline in value then so does your investment portfolio. So does your wealth.

When there is "inflation," the dollar you use to buy things buys less. Your wealth, your future, is in peril.

"The first panacea for a mismanaged nation is inflation of the currency," Ernest Hemingway famously wrote. "The second is war. Both bring a temporary prosperity; both bring a permanent ruin. But both are the refuge of political and economic opportunists."[27]

CHAPTER 4

HERE COMES
THE BOOM

*The US government has a technology, called a printing press,
that allows it to produce as many US dollars as it wishes at
essentially no cost.*

—Ben Bernanke

For the first two decades of the twenty-first century, money had become "easy." On November 21, 2002, the then-Federal Reserve Governor Ben Bernanke gave an address before the National Economists Club in Washington, DC. The speech has come to be known as "The Helicopter Theory" speech—in which Bernanke outlined an economic recipe to avert Japan-style deflation in the United States through a series of tax cuts and low interest rates that could effectively drop cash into the hands of consumers, as if from a helicopter. The result: inflation. Problem solved. Later he would win a Nobel Prize for his work.

If you listen to Bernanke and his successors today, they are still patting themselves on the back. In their view, when consumers refinance their homes and increase their mortgage debt, that frees up money. That money is used to spend and, according to the Fed chairman, that is a good thing—even though the US consumer savings rate had dropped to 2.4% in July of 2022,[1] significantly lower than the inflation rate that month of 8.5%.[2]

When we say things like "people are living paycheck to paycheck," it's because our consumer culture accommodates spending over saving. The Fed, Treasury, and Congress do not encourage savings. Career politicians don't even think about things like the national savings rate. Why would they? Their incentives are to get more for their constituents from the public treasury. The more they can bring home from Washington, the better their chances of getting re-elected. It's perverse.

Unfortunately, the economy and its growing deficits can be forecast by looking at a parallel situation in the late 1990s in one of our Asian trading partners. Japan, even with its work ethic and competitive spirit, discovered the hard way that deficit spending doesn't grow an economy. Deficits, however, are a good way to destroy one.

BIG IN JAPAN

Indeed, we would be wise to heed the lessons of the Japanese experience.[3] We can learn a great deal about what is happening to our dollar today by reviewing the details of the "yen miracle." It was true when we first wrote those words in 2005. It's still true now.

Nearly two decades ago, in 1997, Japan went through an experience that proves the economic wisdom that weak economies have weak currencies and strong economies have strong currencies. This may seem obvious, but we see over and over that economists do not always accept this wisdom. While Greenspan, then our Fed head, said he was concerned with the possible connection between a weakened US dollar and the prospects for the overall economy, his actions weren't convincing.

What the Japan experience showed was that when a country's economy is weakened, it doesn't take much to push it over the edge. After years of growth in its gross domestic product (GDP), the numbers began slowing down. The slowdown was tied to ever-higher budget deficits. By 1997, Japan was in trouble. That year, the government made modest cuts to its budget deficit, and the result was an economic free fall in 1998. GDP fell, inflation followed, and productivity slowed. In response, the government instituted record levels of deficit spending in a Greenspan-esque hope that deficit spending would fix a failing economy. But that same year, the Japanese economy, by all measurements, just got worse and worse.

By 1999, according to the Organization for Economic Cooperation and Development (OECD), restructuring was being promoted as "fortification" for the Japanese economy, but its effect would be doubtful:

> Firms have been making claims that they intend to . . . restructure their businesses. The number of restructuring announcements has surged. . . . But there is a legitimate concern . . . whether [restructuring will be] carried out . . . or whether [share buybacks] are being trotted out for the hoped-for favorable effect on the share price. . . . Many restructuring announcements lack any target for cost cutting by which they can be judged.[4]

> As a matter of fact, it's doubtful that this attempt at restructuring was really helpful to the Japanese economy. It has not grown its way out of its economic and financial imbalances. In fact, the various financial stimulus packages have been ineffective. Between 1992 and 1999, the Japanese government launched 10 such packages, but during the same period its debt grew by $1.13 trillion. The Japanese government policy was premised on the idea that it is possible to spend a country's way out of economic trouble. The numbers prove this theory wrong.

The ratio of government debt to GDP soared from about 60% in 1992 to 105% of GDP in 1999. That is troubling for any economy involved in trade, such as Japan, China, or the United States. The Japanese history lesson reveals that you can't spend your way out of trouble.[5]

Even so, the theme—the official story, if you will—was that Japan's restructuring has fixed the problem. Many of those once-popular international mutual funds bought the story and went through a transitional period, moving investment dollars out of Europe and into Japan. We saw once again—as we have seen so many times in our own domestic stock market—an institutional herd mentality. If everyone is investing in Japan, we can't ignore it. We have to be there too.

Selling business restructuring as the fix was effective, at least in terms of raising foreign investment levels. But restructuring is not the same as investment. Moving debt around and changing its face doesn't fix the problem of deficit spending—a fact the US Fed has not yet learned. We may read all about Japan's promising plans for improving its economy, but the numbers don't support the claimed successes.

The chronic budget deficits coupled with very low interest rates held back any prospects of a real recovery. In fact, conditions in Japan during the 1990s were very similar to conditions in the United States today—and it's a mistake for US policy makers to believe that we are immune from the same outcome that Japan has experienced.

To this day, the Japanese economy is weak and remains chronically so. The country has seen strong GDP growth, low inflation, and climbing exports. The economic fundamental indicators are positive as well: a very high savings rate, strong balance of payments, and virtually no inflation. Even so, Japan's economy refuses to jump-start. Why?[6]

To understand what is going on in Japan—and by association, what may take place in the United States—it's helpful to compare Japan in the 1990s to the United States before the crash of 1929.

The question is debated even today: Was the collapse of the market and of the 1929 economy inevitable? We know of the economic, business, and market excesses of the 1920s, so the unregulated environment was one possible culprit. But was there more? Was the market crash (and the Great Depression that followed) the result of US monetary policies before, during, or after the crash? Could looser money policies have avoided the economic problems?

Probably not.

From a monetary perspective, Japan is the greatest paradox in the world—strong indicators, but a chronically weak economy. Compare this to the United States, where our ever-falling economic indicators have not affected our dollar's value; in fact, we're dealing with a very strong dollar (more on that later).

Japan has the lowest interest rates of any industrialized nation, nearly zero; yet credit growth is the slowest in the world. Is this sluggish expansion a cause or effect of the economy's doldrums?

These doldrums remain troubling. In the face of chronic budget deficits, Japan has not been able to fix its economic pace. The economic policies and business practices are sound, investment and savings rates are high, and exports are surplus. Perhaps Japan's deficits simply got too large and all of the other economic positive signs simply haven't been enough to fix the budget problem. So what does this mean for the United States, where consumer credit increases every year at ever-faster rates, trade deficits are higher than ever, and federal budget deficits are climbing too?

DENIAL IS NOT JUST A RIVER IN EGYPT

Unfortunately for the US consumer, our Fed guy, Ben Bernanke, was not confronting the root of the problem with any proposed solutions during his tenure.

He did keep rates low.

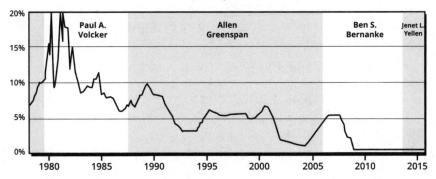

Federal Funds Target Rate

Source: nytimes.com

Free Money for Everyone!

Source: https://www.nytimes.com/interactive/2015/12/11/business/economy/fed-interest-rates-history.html

That flat line on the right existed for nearly a decade before the pandemic hit. In deflation, Ben Bernanke saw a foe he didn't like and chose inflation instead. The result threw us back to inflation rates that Paul Volcker had to deal with in the early Reagan presidency. Here we are, "the greenback boogie." Since 1971, each Fed chairman has had to deal with the previous Fed's theory and strategy. The only real loser in the game is those who have to manage their own money or businesses in a world where they don't get a say or even understand what lies behind the value of their money.

Back when this cycle began in 2010, real productivity had been flat and rising employment numbers represented a shift out of manufacturing and into low-paying health care and retail jobs. That trend only accelerated during the pandemic. No one can know for certain how much more of this kind of productivity the American economy could afford. After all, it worked until it broke.

Like our own Jerome Powell today, Bernanke saw controlling inflation as the centerpiece of economic balance. But he contradicted his claims by pursuing policies that hurt the dollar. That's inflation. But even if we were to have bought into the Fed's "two-part" economic theory, it did not pan out.

Bernanke's theory of low interest rates had a cause-and-effect ideal that went something like this: Low inflation is an opportunity to print new money and to create ever-growing levels of consumer debt. Consumer debt leads to more consumer spending, and more spending is the same thing as prosperity.

Et voilà, you can now spend your way to wealth.

Well, a shot of whiskey is enjoyable and makes us feel good. But if we drink enough shots in one evening, it can kill us. Or call them quantitative easing (QE) martinis. How much credit growth could we really afford? A conservative economic theory would limit credit growth so that it would never exceed savings. Putting this another way, we should never allow our liabilities to exceed our assets.

The economist Stephanie Kelton became the poster child for a theory known as modern monetary theory (MMT). My mentor, Bill Bonner, used to say on occasion "markets make opinions." Stephanie's idea, and others who agree, is that the United States can print all the money it wants, as long as it has the authority to collect it back in tax receipts. That idea can only exist by virtue of the dollar being the reserve currency of the world. And the fact that not a lot a people question policy makers. What MMT effectively does is give politicians and lobbyists a blank check on the nation's bounty. We'll see that play out in spectacular fashion during the COVID-19 pandemic when the Treasury starts sending checks directly to citizens. Why, we always want to ask, are we okay with these decisions? Maybe with a bout of serious inflation, when people are struggling with mortgages, tuition, car loans, gas, and everyday food, we won't be. Maybe the policy makers will start sending free money to people again. At what point does the money become worth less or completely worthless?

In the days prior to Greenspan-Bernanke Fed policy, then Yellen by extension, it was almost universally recognized that it was a function of credit to transfer financial resources from savers to borrowers; an orderly, predictable, and controlled aspect of "leveraging" assets. But the idea that credit could run unchecked above and beyond those assets was thought to be irresponsible—and it is. With rates at zero, banks don't pay savers anything. Anyone who grew up in this era has no idea what savings can or should do. Ideally, your money should be used as a productive asset that pays you back over time. There aren't a lot of people who think that way anymore. Some entrepreneurs, maybe.

The idea of runaway credit is a corollary to another piece of perceived fiscal wisdom: control over interest rates can speed up or slow down the economy. Why were interest rates kept artificially low? There is a good reason. It was not based on purchasing coming from savings, nor from limitations on circulation of currency. It was an attempt to mitigate deflation of the economy during a downturn that was never allowed to happen.

Clearly, the Fed was unwilling to recognize that there is only one real source of growth: a healthy and competitive environment involving the exchange of goods and services coupled with control over deficit spending at the government level. The flaw we identified in the Japanese economy in the 1990s was a failure to eliminate deficit spending that ultimately held down the Japanese economy even when other economic attributes were strong.

TOO MUCH INFORMATION (TMI)

If you listen to explanations from the Fed around that time, you will conclude that the source of strength in the US economy comes from three sources: First, we lead the world in information technology (IT, or what we call "Big Tech" nowadays); second, our free market entrepreneurial culture and the profit motive are unparalleled; third, the US labor market has great flexibility. These might all be true.

The trouble is, the effects of these three features, or what we may collectively call our can-do attitude and Yankee know-how, are exaggerated by the Fed. And the US arrogance shows through. When we look at actual performance by sector, we do not find a profit miracle, nor do we find expanding, competitive manufacturing. We see production jobs going overseas, the expansion of low-paying jobs, and the overall replacement of productive GDP growth with a different kind of GDP, that produced from consumer spending rather than from profitability. That's only a problem when interest rates rise. Companies that count on consumer spending for revenue start feeling the pinch.

The United States has been giving away the capability to manufacture goods based on innovative technology for years and failing to compete in markets that are aggressively (and successfully) going after market share. That tide may be changing. But it's difficult for individual investors to understand and act proactively. Currently, macropolitical trends are in place too. The Russia-Ukraine war is causing all the energy markets in the world to get flummoxed. Chip makers in Taiwan are getting a rash, too, from the People's Party in mainland China. Both markets—energy and microchips—fuel and function the world. No hyperbole needed.

We can look at a promising short-term trend in Big Tech and call it an indicator of sorts. In fact it was only a bubble. And another bubble. Then another one. We talk more extensively about bubbles in our next revised book, *Financial Reckoning Day*. What we can say here of bubbles is that they are often propelled by a new technology. They capture the imagination of the public and cause fits and seizures in the marketplace. Some people make money. Most don't.

American businesses have not kept their lead, and like other manufacturing sectors of our economy, they're losing to China and India—and other places around the world—almost as quickly as credit card debt is increasing. The onetime encouragement to "buy American" isn't possible any longer because so many of the products we purchase (like shoes, electronics, computers, and denim jeans, for example) are being manufactured in China, India, and other Asian and Central American countries. So no one can "buy American" any longer. Today, your only choice is to "spend American." Or fly American.

FICTITIOUS CAPITALISM

This drastic change in how the US economy works may be accurately described as the replacement of real capitalism with show-business fictitious capitalism. We already know from looking at the numbers that the applauded twentieth century "Information Age" didn't really create an American economic miracle. The overall effect was not a big splash, and it represented too small a share of GDP to count as a major trend. It was more like a short-term indicator that was contradicted by the larger economic trend—leading us toward spending. Between 2002 and 2007, for example, spending on information technology and hardware hovered around 2% of GDP, but no more: It is now less than 1% of GDP.

The most significant indicator in our economy was not productivity, but expansion of credit. Under Greenspan's term, US credit and debt added up to $8.505 trillion. That means it took $4.80 of new debt to create one dollar of GDP. And then, with the burden of US credit and debt up to $9.149 trillion under his successor, Ben Bernanke, it took more than $5 to create one dollar of GDP. Every additional dollar in credit adds a dollar to someone's debt—yours, mine, the government's, or, realistically, the debt of future generations of American taxpayers and consumers.

How did all this so-called "disposable income" develop? The housing bubble. Homeowners were able to take out their equity and increase their debt at ever-lower interest rates. This lopsided switch away from production and toward debt is at the heart of the demise of the dollar. Americans no longer have gobs of equity to spend. But we're used to spending, so then what happens?

In the less than two years with Bernanke, our credit expanded from $3 trillion to $3.3 trillion. But a funny thing happened in November 2007: Credit dropped by nearly 9%, back down to $3 trillion. Maybe the rest of the world is sick and tired of our addiction to cheap credit.

Globally, central banks dumped about $163 billion in US Treasuries. Not since Russia's 1998 default have US Treasuries been sold at such a pace. And these numbers are from September 2007—before the Fed cut the overnight rate not once, but five times by January 30, 2008.

NET WORTHLESS

"History shows," wrote Jim Rogers in the foreword to our first book, *Financial Reckoning Day* (John Wiley & Sons, 2003), "that people who save and invest grow and prosper, and the others deteriorate and collapse." Business investment creates economic recoveries. Without that investment, we have no right to expect a recovery. Except we've seen over the past decade and a half that free money has been available and the corporate community and Wall Street have interpreted the influx of capital as success.

The Fed and other monetary gurus claim that the low level of business investment is to be blamed on excess inventories and low demand overseas, or some such blame on the supply chain issues caused by the pandemic lockdowns. Realistically, corporate America has gone through a trend in the past two decades in which dwindling profits have led to increased levels of mergers and acquisitions, but little change in the lagging profit picture. The belief, or the hope, that merging and internal cost cutting would solve profitability problems has been dashed. It hasn't worked. The pandemic only muddied the picture more.

Corporate America is coming to the point of having to face its own set of realities. Merging does not improve profits if the market itself is weak. Buy backs don't necessarily work either. This is the point of the term "fictitious capitalism." You can buy and sell paper all day, but if you're not producing anything, you're not producing anything. No one seems to really care about that. Lacking real investment in plant and equipment, long-term growth is less likely today than before the merger mania, buy backs, or the growing trade deficit. We have been writing about this for years. Coupled with an expanding obligation for pension liabilities among large corporations, the problem of deceptive reporting isn't limited to the government. Corporations do the same thing. We're not complaining; the situation is just real.

Consider the following: Many corporations notoriously inflate their earnings report. Quite legitimately, and with the blessings of the accounting industry, companies exclude many big expense items from their operating statements and may include revenues that should be left out. Exclusions like employee stock option expenses can be huge.

At the same time, including estimated earnings from future invest-ments of pension plan assets is only an estimate and cannot be called reliable. Standard & Poor's (the revered S&P) has devised a method for making adjustments to arrive at a company's core earnings. Those are the earnings from the primary business of the company, and anything reported should be recurring.

The adjustments aren't small. For example only, and as a historical example, when we were covering the story in 2002, E.I. du Pont de Nemours (DuPont) reported earnings of more than $5 billion based on an audited statement and in compliance with all of the rules. But when adjustments were made to arrive at core earnings, the $5 billion profit was reduced to a $347 million loss; core earnings adjustments that year of nearly $5.5 billion had to be made. That is a big change. Other big negative adjustments had to be made that year for IBM ($5.7 billion reported profits versus $287 million in core earnings) and General Motors ($1.8 billion reported profits versus a $2.4 billion core loss). That year, the two largest core earnings adjustments were made by Citicorp ($13.7 billion in adjustments) and General Electric ($11.2 billion in adjustments).[7]

Here's where the question of realistic net worth comes into play: In accounting, any adjustment made in earnings has to have an offset somewhere. So when Citicorp over-reports its earnings by $13.7 bil-lion, that means it has also understated its liabilities by the same amount—a fact that should be very troubling to stockholders. One of the largest of the core earnings adjustments is unfunded pension plan liabilities. United Airlines, for example, announced in 2004 that it was going to stop funding pension contributions. After filing Chapter 11 bankruptcy in 2002, the United Airlines unfunded liability is an esti-mated $6.4 billion.[8]

When we hear that a corporation has not recorded employee stock option expenses of $1 billion, that also means the company's net worth is exaggerated by the same amount—and the book value of the company is exaggerated. So all of the numbers investors depend on are simply wrong. The escalating pension woes have been building up for years. It's a similar challenge the government faces when it keeps adding deficits to the mounting debt; they're effectively kicking the can down the road.

A booming stock market adds to corporate profits. But once the market retreated, those profits disappear. In this situation, stock prices fall while ongoing pension liabilities rise. As employees retire, obligatory payments have to be made out of operating profits and—while few corporate types want to talk about this—those very pension obligations and depressed returns on invested assets may be a leading factor in a high number of corporate bankruptcies. Add on a challenging retail sales environment during rising interest rates or wholesale price issues caused by supply chain disruptions—both a result of pandemic lockdowns—filing for bankruptcy often becomes the only way out when the corporations cannot afford to meet their pension obligations.

A PENNY BORROWED IS A PENNY EARNED

The US economy is based on the belief that in practice, borrowing is a type of wealth generation. The trouble is . . . it's not. Economic policy and growth are going to reflect how consumers spend what they have, individually and as a nation. The critical question to ask is: How much of our overall current production is devoted to consumption and how much to capital investment? In defining economic health and strength, generations of economists have focused on two economic indicators: savings and investment. It used to be a truism among economists of all schools of thought that the growth of an economy's tangible capital stock was the key determinant of increased productivity and subsequently of good, high-paying jobs. And it also used to be a truism that tangible capital investment in factories, production equipment, and commercial and residential building represents the one and only form of genuine wealth creation.

Not so anymore. The United States has abandoned these beliefs, even though they are obvious and, well, true. The laws of economics haven't been revoked, but the wonks in Washington behave as if they have.

To Americans, the suggestion that the dollar is losing value is unthinkable—unpatriotic even. The problem is found not only in the lack of understanding about the nature of wealth and the investments used to create and sustain it; in our money culture, policy makers and economists make no distinction between wealth created through saving and investment in the real economy versus "wealth" created in the markets through asset bubbles brought about by credit policies. Even when suggestions about the flaw in this thinking arise, the distraction of consumerism has created a type of attention deficit disorder. We're trying to tell people to lose weight while meeting with them for lunch at the soda fountain.

We not only spend at a high level; we also prefer accumulating wealth on the same fast track. Traditionally, economists recognized that it took time to build an estate. People and countries could build wealth slowly. But today

> the new approach requires that a state find ways to increase the market value of its productive assets. [In such a strategy] an economic policy that aims to achieve growth by wealth creation therefore does not attempt to increase the production of goods and services, except as a secondary objective.[9]

This is a perfect description of the economic thinking that rules in the United States today, not only in corporations and the financial markets, but even among policy makers, elevating wealth creation—that is, bubble creation—to the ultimate in economic wisdom. The asset bubbles in recent years—in stocks, bonds, and housing—were primary elements of economic growth. Considering, though, the lopsided effect on consumer spending and borrowing, is this a reasonable and sustainable policy? Should it be encouraged? It works in the short run from the demand side, but where does it lead? Just as mercantilism in eighteenth-century Europe ultimately fell under its own weight, the modern economic trend toward house-of-cards wealth creation may become a twenty-first-century version of past lessons not fully learned or appreciated.

America's grinding credit machine makes all the difference in economic growth and wealth creation between our country and the rest of the world. Lately, China is overtaking the United States in so many ways, but, ironically, based on a more tangible economic viewpoint. It may prove to be the great irony of the twenty-first century that the Chinese—once viewed as the most puristic of the Communist regimes, rabidly anticapitalist at the height of their fervor—may turn out to be the most successful model of worldwide capitalism. (On a recent trip to China, I had a good chuckle while touring the Forbidden Palace in Beijing. The tour was sponsored by Nestlé, and the plaques that explained where the concubines slept had American Express logos in the lower-right corners.)

China's growth is no laughing matter. It is investment-driven, with a capital investment rate close to 43% of GDP in 2006. GDP growth increased to 10.7% that year, and then rose by 11.1% in the first quarter of 2007. But the country's investment rate isn't the only record—in 2005, personal saving reached 52% of GDP, according to an envious US Treasury. By US standards, that is very, very high.

SERIAL BUBBLE BLOWERS

According to the consensus view, the US economy is breaking out of its anemic growth pattern. A few signs of accelerating economic improvement are gleefully cited to support this forecast: the 3.9% spurt of "real GDP growth" in the third quarter of 2007; higher investment technology spending, up 9% in 2006; surging profits; and surging early indicators, among them, in particular, indicators such as the Institute for Supply Management (ISM) survey for manufacturing.[10]

We hear that various indicators are at their strongest in 20 years. But do we simply accept the popular wisdom? No, because many of the reported indicators are nonrecurring. If they aren't really signs of a sustained pattern, the results are dubious at best. For example, the impressive third quarter 2003 growth spurt was the direct result of a one-time splurge in federal tax rebates and a flurry of mortgage refinancing caused by low interest rates. In the third quarter of 2007, we had similarly impressive results, GDP growth of 3.9%. But you've got to read between the lines: Growth was fueled by personal consumption, which doubled to over 3%, and export growth in goods, the largest bump up since the fourth quarter of 1996. "Housing values fell, foreclosures accelerated, and imports grew" had become a familiar economic refrain in 2007.

As to investment spending, what is really going on? So-called investment in housing is now distorted by the escalating foreclosures and credit crisis caused by the subprime mortgage mess. What should matter is the change in total nonresidential investment—business factories and equipment, for example—a trend that has been flat for many years. There is no real growth in business investment.

The US economy's so-called improvement has one main reason: All the economic growth of the "recovery" years since 2001 can be traced to a seemingly endless array of asset and borrowing bubbles. Quoting analyst Stephen Roach, "The Fed, in effect, has become a serial bubble blower"—first the stock market bubble, then the bond bubble, then the housing bubble, and the mortgage refinancing bubble. As a result, consumer spending has been surging well in excess of disposable income for years. But we must understand, this is not *real* growth.

The idea behind the bubble economy was that sustained and rising consumer spending would eventually stimulate investment spending. This is like suggesting that overeating will eventually lead to serious dieting. As you might expect, rising consumer spending has not had the desired effect. In fact, consumer spending will slow down when consumer borrowing starts to fade. And that's just a matter of time.

The dollar is going to continue falling over the long run. It will fall as long as we continue to outspend our investment and production rates. If foreign investors were to slash their investment levels in the US dollar and Treasury securities, that would cause a hard landing. Our credit would dry up rapidly. This would not just send the dollar crashing. A sudden rupture of private capital would also hammer the US bond and stock markets.

Private foreign investment into US assets has slumped. But we are addicted to foreign investment; this is where much of our consumer credit and debt is financed. So we are vulnerable if our credit economy is supported primarily by huge holdings of dollars on the part of foreign private and institutional investors. If the dollar's fall begins to frighten foreign owners, they will sell from this immense stock of dollar assets.

How big are these foreign holdings? We rarely hear about this problem on the financial news channels, so what's the big deal? Well, let's run the numbers. By the end of 2006, foreign holdings of US dollars had a market value of $16.295 trillion. This includes corporate and government bonds held directly and by foreign governments. It's a big number. The point here is that these huge foreign dollar holdings are a looming threat to the dollar, perhaps the biggest threat of all. If these foreign investors lose confidence in the US economy and the dollar, they will sell and switch the dollar proceeds into a stronger currency.

That $16.295 trillion is a lot of debt. A lot. How is it going to get repaid? And by whom? The figure in 2022 is much smaller as governments unload their US debt to whomever will buy it. But the process is the same: the Treasury must "roll" the debt over every time a US treasuries term comes due. They do so at auction. If they don't raise enough money at auction to keep the government's lights on, they have to raise interest rates to attract buyers. Financing the government through debt is an ongoing task.

The hope in Washington is that the declining value of the dollar will reduce the US trade deficit. Past experience shows that this is unlikely. The chronic US trade deficit is caused by exceptionally high levels of consumption, undersaving, and underinvestment. Improving the trade deficit would require a major correction of these imbalances and cannot be fixed simply by watching the dollar's value continue to decline.

An economic downturn would come as a rude awakening to most Americans, a cataclysmic shock. It would directly affect the other two asset bubbles, housing and stocks, in addition to the dollar value bubble itself. Imagine the uncertainty and turmoil this will create in the financial markets. Rock solid? We think not.

The US economy is much weaker and much more vulnerable than official statistics make it seem. The Fed cushioned the impact of the bursting stock market bubble by manipulating new asset bubbles. Ultralow short-term interest rates and the promise to keep them there for a long time have fueled a housing and mortgage borrowing boom, which also extended the consumer borrowing-and-spending binge. "Happy days are here again." Indeed.

While European policy makers and economists worry endlessly about budget deficits and slow growth, their counterparts on this side of the pond continue to boast how wonderfully efficient and flexible the US economy is. Negative national savings, a growing trade deficit, never-ending budget deficits, the subprime mortgage mess, and the credit crisis—all these and any other imbalances and dislocations are nonproblems. The official word is that the exploding credit and ballooning debt in the United States are not signs of excess, but a testament to the financial system's extraordinary efficiency.

Small prediction: A shock awaits the "nonproblem" crowd when we finally confront our economic realities. The US inflation rate is understated by at least 1.5 percentage points per year through the economic/statistical magic of grossly overstating real GDP and productivity growth. Bond king Bill Gross discovered this fact of life and commented on it in 2004.[11] An active proponent of inflation manipulation was former Fed chairman Alan Greenspan, apparently because—and here again we find a recurring theme—"a low inflation rate fosters low interest rates."

The huge credit and debt bubbles in the United States have created a dislocated and imbalanced economy, so that a sustained recovery is going to be impossible without many painful changes. We suffer from a false sense of optimism, and when the implicit promise of that optimism is not met, experts will no longer be able to argue away the dollar's weakness.

Under a system of truly free currency markets, the dollar would have collapsed long ago. But the massive dollar purchases by the Asian central banks have prevented this. China's persistence in pegging its currency to the dollar traps other Asian countries into doing the same. This practice creates a credit bubble that, in turn, distorts economic growth. In contrast, the European Central Bank is firmly opposed to currency intervention. In its view, artificial tinkering in the currency markets tends to fuel credit excess. It could be right, using the US economy as an example.

Those who like currency intervention policy—artificially controlling the value of the dollar, in essence—ignore the beneficial effects of a rising currency. The benefit is twofold. First, it reduces the trade deficit and makes us more competitive with our trade partners. Second, it also adds a healthy premium to domestic purchasing power. It's important, though, to make a distinction here. Under our present system, our purchasing power is based exclusively on borrowed money. Under a system of competitive trade and a higher dollar, our purchasing power would be based on real economic forces, and not on good credit alone.

"The lengthy pegging of Asian currencies to the US dollar will eventually lead to an economic crisis in both the United States and Asia," we wrote in 2008, "because the central banks accommodate each other's credit and spending excesses. So we have to change the system so that competitive forces can work and replace currency intervention as international policy." The crisis has arrived in the form of inflation, hastened by the massive economic dislocations wrought by the pandemic lockdowns.

A weakened US economy shouldn't surprise anyone. It is a direct result of the questionable nature of the so-called economic recovery. The US economy is plagued by an array of growth-inhibiting imbalances: the trade deficit, the federal budget deficit, household indebtedness, a negative personal saving rate, and, of course, record-high consumer spending. Any other country faced with these imbalances would have collapsed long ago. But the US dollar was spared this fate when Asian central banks began accumulating the dollars needed to avoid rises in their currencies.

Both the United States and China practice credit excess, but with a crucial difference: In the United States, the credit excesses went into higher asset prices and, more notably, into personal consumption. In Asia, credit excesses went into capital investment and production. The result is an odd disparity between the two economies: Americans borrow and consume, and the Asians produce.

This symbiosis plays out in the trade gap. Ironically, this ever-growing problem is ignored on the national level and plays virtually no role in US economic policy or analysis. Since 1999, the trade deficit as a share of GDP has nearly tripled, from 2.1% to 5.75%. In comparison, during the 1980s, policy makers and economists worried about the harm that trade deficits were causing in US manufacturing. In a September 1985 move orchestrated by James Baker, the US Treasury secretary, the finance ministers of the G-5 nations[127] agreed to drive the dollar sharply down in concerted action.

By the mid-1990s US policy makers had decided that trade deficits were beneficial for the US economy and its financial markets. Cheap imports were playing an important role in preventing inflation and, as a result, higher interest rates. Had the decision been to allow interest rates to rise, it would have had the effect of slowing down consumer spending. Instead, spending is out of control and the trade gap is the consequence. Ultimately, the victim in all of this is going to be the US dollar.

The economic cycle involving inflation, higher interest rates, monetary tightening, recession, and recovery has a predictable postwar pattern in the United States and in the rest of the world. But we've taken a departure from this for the first time. A critic might argue that the United States enjoyed a prolonged period of strong economic growth with low inflation and low interest rates. What could be bad about that?

Well, what's bad about that is the fact that we are *not* experiencing strong economic growth. US net business investment has fallen to all-time postwar lows, little more than 2% of GDP in recent years. At the same time, net financial investment is running at about 7.8% of GDP. In other words, the counterpart to foreign investment in the US economy has been higher private and public consumption, accompanied by lower saving and investment.

Official opinion in America says that the huge US trade gap is mainly the fault of foreigners, for two reasons. One is the eagerness of foreign investors to acquire US assets with higher returns than in the rest of the world; the other is supposed to be weaker economic growth in the rest of the world. In this view, the trade gap directly results from foreign investment because it provides the dollars that the foreign investors need.

A RISING TIDE

Corporate management may have been reined in, to some extent, by changes in federal law (don't tell my libertarian friends I said that). The Sarbanes-Oxley Act of 2002 changed the culture in some important ways. But until the accounting industry goes through some changes of its own, the corporate problem won't disappear. Nothing has really changed since then. It appears so far that the disaster of Arthur Andersen converted to the now acceptable Accenture on August 31, 2002, it has been viewed in the accounting industry as a public relations problem rather than what it really is: a deep, cultural failure within the business to protect the stockholders. It's a PR problem!

The parallels between corporate failures and government policy are alarming, if only because the Fed is not accountable to the Securities and Exchange Commission (SEC) or to stockholders in the same way that corporate chief executive officers and chief financial officers are—and civil fines or imprisonment are out of the question. So as far as accountability is concerned, it looks like the borrowing and spending will continue—with yet more wild abandon.

The half-hearted debate over the twin deficits in trade and budget involve some big numbers, but the Fed is not concerned. In his penchant for understatement, Ben Bernanke was a lot like his old boss, Alan Greenspan. Read what he told the Charlotte, North Carolina, Chamber of Commerce in late November 2007, explaining why the Fed's monetary policy committee, the Federal Open Market Committee (FOMC), decided to cut the short-term interest rate in October:

> Growth appeared likely to slow significantly in the fourth quarter from its rapid third-quarter rate and to remain sluggish in early 2008.[13]

Still, like Greenspan, Bernanke was upbeat, believing that growth would thereafter gradually return to a pace approaching its long-run trend as the drag from housing subsided and financial conditions improved.[14] Although he admits that construction and home sales continued to be "weak," and that the unemployment rate had "drifted up" to 4.7%, he pointed to "solid" gains in the labor market in October. What gains? The 130,000 new jobs added to private-sector payrolls were mostly service and temp jobs. A rate of 4.7% is too close for comfort to 5%, the official mark when an economy is in recession. Then he turned a bit more realistic, admitting the combination of higher gas prices, the weak housing market, tighter credit conditions, and "declines in stock prices seem likely to create some headwinds for the consumer in the months ahead."[15] Sound familiar? Headwinds! That's a nice way of saying we're headed for stormy weather.

> The fresh wave of investor concern has contributed in recent weeks to a decline in equity values, a widening of risk spreads for many credit products (not only those related to housing), and increased short-term funding pressures. These developments have resulted in a further tightening in financial conditions, which has the potential to impose additional restraint on activity in housing markets and in other credit-sensitive sectors.[16]

Analyze this for reality, taken from the burning pages of the *Daily Reckoning:*

> The credit bubble wouldn't have gotten so large were it not for the Fed. The Fed guarantees the solvency of the credit markets like Fannie Mae guarantees the solvency of the mortgage-backed security market. . . . Without Fannie Mae, mortgage-lending practices wouldn't have gotten crazy. . . . Without the Fed, the issuance of collateralized debt obligations (a type of asset-backed security that is as dubious as it sounds, funding portfolio investments with credit-risky, fixed-income assets) wouldn't have mushroomed. . . .
>
> "A rising tide lifts all fortunes," promises the saying—but not with this extreme form addiction to risky credit. Under terms of the agreement hammered out with lenders, only a fraction of an estimated 2.3 million subprime borrowers—an estimated 145,000–240,000 borrowers—will qualify for the freeze.

As borrowing increased as a percentage of GDP—up to more than 70% during the 1980s—savings rates fell and continued falling. By the end of the 1990s, borrowing had reached 90% of GDP, and reached 95% less than a decade later, in 2006. That's where the real damage was done. And in the middle of the very same trend, non-financial business profits fell as well. The so-called US expansion had, in fact, been a nonexpansion. Corporate profits, which fell in the 1980s from 5.1% of GDP down to 3.7%, continued their downward spiral. By definition, a profitless expansion is not really an expansion at all. The bubble economy of the 1980s was the beginning of a worsening effect in real numbers that built throughout the 1990s and beyond.

MR. IRRATIONAL EXUBERANCE

Alan Greenspan, the longtime chairman of the Federal Reserve, set us on this runaway course. "Mr. Irrational Exuberance"[17] himself set the standard for twenty-first century American monetary policy with the mantra: "In debt? No problem. Spend more money—we'll print it for you."

Greenspan was followed consecutively by Ben Bernanke who had made himself famous on his way up the ladder for giving a speech claiming the Fed had the tools to get money into consumers hands like "piles of cash being thrown out of a helicopter."

In late October 2006, Bernanke voted with the rest of the FOMC—the Fed's policy-making arm—to cut interest rates for the third month in a row. He was not, as the financial press called him early in his tenure, the "un-Greenspan." Rather, Bernanke was the reincarnation of Mr. Irrational Exuberance.

In his autobiography, *The Age of Turbulence,* published by Penguin Press in September 2007, Greenspan said he thought it wrong to increase scrutiny of subprime mortgages. Call me cynical, but increased scrutiny might have helped; 52% of these risky mortgages, made to borrowers with poor credit histories, were originated by companies and organizations with zero federal supervision. "I really didn't get it until very late in 2005 and 2006," Greenspan told Reuters in an interview, apologizing for the insane housing bubble he helped create, which led to the subprime mortgage mess and the credit crisis.

In the third and fourth quarters of 2007, Citigroup ($11.38 billion), Merrill Lynch ($8.48 billion), Morgan Stanley ($4.68 billion), and Barclays ($2.7 billion) led the pack in write-downs—government-approved losses on these loans.

By October 2008, the US Commerce Department reported that housing permits fell to a 14-year low, the lowest seasonally adjusted level since July 1993. In distressed markets such as San Francisco, home builders shaved off as much as $150,000 from prices. And foreclosures nearly doubled (94%) from October 2006 to October 2007. "We have not seen a nationwide decline in housing like this since the Great Depression," said Wells Fargo chief executive John Stumpf, who correctly foresaw the crisis swallowing the market a year later. "I don't think we're in the ninth inning of unwinding this," he said in 2007, "If we are, it's going to be an extra-inning game."

Stumpf was right, unfortunately. As were the characters portrayed in the financial tome turned box office hit, *The Big Short*. By the time the year wound down, sales of new homes had plummeted 26.4%, according to the US Department of Commerce—the worst slump since 1980. And housing starts fell almost as hard, by 24.8%. *BusinessWeek,* before it was bought out by Bloomberg, summed up the state of the nation in 2007: "The Economy on the Edge."[18]

It is worth noting that Bernanke won the Nobel Prize in Economics in 2022 for his work following the global financial crisis of 2008–2009. Whether you agree with his methods or not, one thing is for sure: He made decisions during those years to change the course of monetary policy for decades to come. We are still dealing with the "better capitalized" banks he described at the podium in Norway. "They should be better prepared to meet whatever challenges they face," he continued. Keyword should. Books will be (and have been) written about Bernanke, but that's not our objective here. We're all about the money.

CHAPTER 5

OOPS, HERE'S
THE BUST

History reminds us that dictators and despots arise during times of severe economic crisis.

—*Robert Kiyosaki*

Bernanke's policy did not bring about a "recovery" in 2008–2009 as it was often heralded. In fact, then-Treasury Secretary Hank Paulsen's big bank bailouts were just fuel on the fire. We call it "papering" over a problem. Print more money. Quantitative easing. Call it what you want, the American government began buying private assets off the market to prop up bank earnings and create the illusion of recovery. This period of artificial stimulation is the net cause of the historic inflation we experienced globally in 2022.

And now it is Jerome Powell's job to clean up the magma-hot cinders. Some might even say that the global economy has yet to undo the effects of such "cheap money." The dollar has been teetering between deflation and inflation. But before the demise of the dollar can be arrested, the causes—runaway debt and US government policy—must be addressed. In targeting "deflation" for so many years following the 2008 financial panic, the Fed actually created another one: an inflationary panic. To fight what they perceived to be a deflationary environment, the Fed left interest rates at zero for six years, from 2009–2015, all prior to the pandemic, an historic period of easy money.

In the past, US recessions arose from cheap money and excess credit. So here we go again. It's a feature, or a bug, of the Great Dollar Standard Era that the Federal Reserve has to pull levers and push buttons, publish the minutes to their FOMC meetings, and hold press releases to signal the banks what's coming down the road, direct traders on Wall Street what to buy and when and thereby "control" the economy. All for nigh? Hopefully our work here is helpful enough so you understand and don't have to worry about it. . . too much.

THE R-WORD(S)

So what is a "recession," anyway? According to the National Bureau of Economic Research (NBER)—the official recession scorekeeper—a recession is "a significant decline in economic activity that is spread across the economy and that lasts more than a few months."[1] Of course, it takes time for the NBER to compile the data, so a common guffaw among writers in the financial space is the NBER will tell us we were in a recession well after the recovery is underway.

Most normal people think of a recession in terms of lost jobs, which is only one aspect of the bigger picture which involves difficulty in getting loans for homeowners, car buyers, and small businesses, and students trying to pay tuition.

The theory the Fed operates on, as we've seen aggressively in 2022, is that it can raise interest rates and squash demand for goods and services in the economy. A "recession" will slow down the economy, rein in inflation, and bring the financial system back into balance. The unnatural phenomenon here is that a recession is not necessarily something that has arisen naturally. When you pump money into the system, each dollar becomes less valuable. The only tool the Fed has to slay inflation is to dampen economic activity.

It's a necessary evil in the Fed's eyes. Its goal is to keep inflation in check by crushing consumer demand, meaning it wants to slow down people's desire to spend money. That's nuts. People change their spending habits based on the signals they get from the media and the like before the economy retreats.

Cutting back on credit when recession occurs is a form of economic dieting. We have to slim down as a result of tight money so that the economy can get back into those tight jeans it wore last summer. Most of us know exactly what that is like and what it means.

Thing is something has changed in the United States. Our economy is fast becoming morbidly obese, and we have long abandoned the desire to slim down. We just keep buying bigger and bigger expectations. We've been living in the bubble. And it's about to pop.

It became official economic policy under Alan Greenspan's tenure with the Fed not only to accept but to actually encourage borrowing and spending excesses. This occurs under the respectable label of "wealth-driven" spending.

When we speak at conferences and talk to people around the country, we're consistently surprised at how little people actually know about the money they pack away in their wallets. Since 1913 and the passage of the Federal Reserve Act, the federal government has ceded the power over money expressly given to it by the Constitution to private interests. Article I of our Constitution gives Congress the power to coin money and to regulate its value. But that power has been delegated to the Fed, which is essentially a banking cartel and *not* part of Congress. This isn't just politics or stuffy economics. By allowing the Fed to have this power, we have no direct voice in how monetary policy is set, not that it would do much good anyway. The loss of sound money—money backed by a tangible asset rather than a government process—is the root imbalance that's plaguing the dollar.

To give you an idea of how the recession and recovery trend has changed, look at the historical numbers—the real numbers, not the political/economic numbers we are being fed. Early in 2007, President George W. Bush released a budget in which the ledger shifted from red to black and showed a nice surplus of $61 billion, by 2012. But—and this is a big but—it assumed real government spending growth of 0.4% a year. Bush racked up real growth at the rate of 4.6% since he took office in 2001, compared with 2.7% under Ronald Reagan and 0.8% under Bill Clinton. As the Federal Reserve Bank of Dallas wrote in April 2007, "Washington's fiscal fitness remains a matter of concern. . . . The most recent proposal envisions eliminating them [budget deficits] within six years, but doing so will require lawmakers to overcome several significant obstacles."[2]

And we all know, unfortunately, that's not likely to happen, given the fiscal leadership we've seen so far.

The peak-to-trough changes shown in past recessions make the point: We're not gaining and losing economic weight and returning to previous health in the same way; something has changed drastically and, like a Florida sinkhole, we're slowly going under.

That's why the dollar crisis is invisible. We really don't want to think about it, and the Fed enables us to ignore it by telling us that all is well. As long as credit card companies keep giving us more cards and increasing our credit limits, why worry? And that, in a nutshell, defines the economic problem behind the demise.

An economist would shrug off these changes as cyclical or simply as signs that in the latest recovery a bias toward consumption is affecting outcome. But what does that mean? If, in fact, we are no longer willing to accept tight money as a reality in the down part of the economic cycle, how can we sustain economic growth? How much is going to be enough? And what will happen when seemingly infinite credit and debt excesses finally catch up with us?

AMERICAN MONEY

The United States has a lot of wealth, but that wealth is being consumed very quickly. History shows that no matter how rich you are, you can lose that wealth if you're not productive. Meanwhile, the dollar's value falls and—in spite of the Fed's view that this is a good thing—it means our savings are worth less. Your spending power falls when the dollar falls, and as this continues, the consequences will be sobering.

The dollar's plunge has taken many people, currency experts of banks included, by surprise. For many of them, it is still impossible to grasp. A talking head on CNBC said that he was at a complete loss to understand how such weak economies as those seen in the European Union could have a strong currency. For American policy makers and most economists, the huge trade deficit is no problem. They find it natural that fast-growing countries import money while slow-growing economies export money. At least, that is the recurring theme.

So Americans traveling abroad may continue to complain that "it has become so expensive to travel in Europe" as though the problem were somehow the fault of the Europeans. But in fact, it is the declining spending power of the dollar that is to blame, and not just the French, the Italians, and the residents of the so-called chocolate-making countries.

This problem is pegged not to some speculative or fuzzy economic cause, even though the concept of currency exchange rates continues to mystify. A historically large trade deficit is at the core of the declining dollar. Somebody needs to get over the notion that our economy is strong and other economies are weak, merely because this is America. In the United States, the reason for the trade deficit is not a high rate of investment as we see in some other countries, but an abysmally low level of national savings. We are spending, not producing.

A second argument offered by some is that "capital flows from high-saving countries to low-saving countries, wanting to grow faster." Under this reasoning, a deficit country, looking at both consumption and investment, is absorbing more than its own production. But whether this is good or bad for the economy depends on the source and use of foreign funds. Do those funds pay for the financing of consumption in excess of production (as in the United States) or for investment in excess of saving? That is the key question that ought to be asked in the first place about the huge US capital imports.

To quote Joan Robinson, a well-known economist in the 1920s and 1930s who was close to John Maynard Keynes:

> If the capital inflows merely permit an excess of consumption over production, the economy is on the road to ruin. If they permit an excess of investment over home saving, the result depends on the nature of the investment.[3]

The huge US capital inflows (economic jargon for money coming into the country), accounting now for more than 6% of GDP, have not financed productive investment; in fact, they are financing more and more debt. Capital grew from 5% in 2005 to more than 6% in 2006, according to a report from the Bureau of Economic Analysis (BEA), "US International Investment Position." Our net investments are among the lowest in the world, meaning we prefer spending and borrowing over actual production and growth. The huge capital inflows have not helped finance a higher rate of investment. The United States has been selling its factories and financial assets to pay for consumption.

It's helpful to use a real means for measuring economic strength. Money coming here from overseas finances higher personal consumption. The steep decline in personal saving is a symptom of our spending, and along with that habit we have lower capital investment and a growing federal budget deficit. In the third quarter of 2005, for the first time ever, the rate actually fell into negative territory—to −1%.

The US economy has for years been the strongest in the world, leading the rest of the countries. Our *Daily Reckoning* newsletter routinely gets reader responses saying, in effect, "How dare you impugn the superiority of the American economy! How dare you!" We're rather thick-skinned, so the insults bounce off rather easily. But facts are stubborn things. The fact that the US economy has outperformed the rest of the world in the past several years is easily explained: Our credit machine has been operating in overdrive nonstop. It is geared to accommodate unlimited credit for two purposes—consumption and financial speculation. Let's look at these two things a little more deeply.

Credit is not the same thing as production, despite the fuzzy logic you get from the financial media. There is a severe imbalance between the huge amount of credit that goes into the economy and the minimal amount that goes into productive investment. Instead of moving to rein in these excesses and imbalances, under Greenspan, The Fed clearly opted to sustain and even to encourage them. Under the tenure of Bernanke, and Yellen following, we wanted to believe the Fed would do better.

Alas, by 2021, Jerome Powell had to contend with a decade of below-market, Fed-set interest rates. Low interest rates encouraged increased consumer spending on credit cards and jumbo mortgages often beyond borrowers' means. Low interest rates also disincentivized saving. These economic behaviors became habitual. The average American, while feeling as though they were getting more wealthy were really benefiting from an extended era of cheap money.[4]

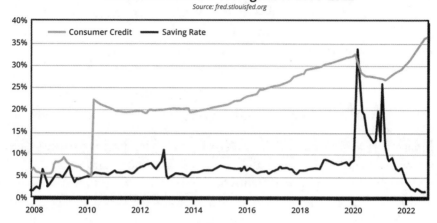

Consumer Credit v. Savings Rate 2008–2022
Source: fred.stlouisfed.org

FIGURE 5.1 Consumer Credit Versus Savings Rate
Source: St. Louis Fed, fred.stlouisfed.org

You can see the spike in 2010 of consumer credit as rates were historically low. They sustained high levels until 2020, while the savings rate stayed relatively steady. The real cravings caused by the nation's credit habit began to show during 2022. As the Powell Fed got serious about fighting inflation, raising interest rates at the most aggressive pace in the Fed's history, consumers began to get squeezed. Inflation was causing consumers to use credit as a way to keep up their spending. Savings, which were already low, plummeted. (See Figure 5.1).

Low interest rates spurred a decade-long frenzy of financial speculation too, which is equally unproductive. An "investor" puts up capital to generate a sustained and long-term growth plan. For example, buying and holding stocks is a form of investment and a sign that the investor has faith in the management of that company.

"Speculators" don't care about long-term growth. They want to get in and out of positions as quickly as possible, make a profit, and repeat the process. Instead of investing money to produce a product, they're interested in taking advantage of price anomalies in the market. They trade paper, not goods. So speculative profits—especially those paid for with borrowed money—tend to be churned over and over in further speculation and increased spending. None of that money goes into investment in the long-term sense. The speculator is invested in short-term profits, nothing more. Even so, the speculator is today's cowboy, the risk-taking, living-on-the-edge market hero willing to take big chances. He is seen as a guy with big stones because he's staring the prospect of loss right in the eye.

MAKING LESS THAN DAD

Inflation is a hard nut to crack. Most people in the job market have grown up with the expectation they'll make more and more as life and experience accumulate. Is it true?

The riddle of the next recession is not necessarily an economic one. Recessions happen. The riddle is how the next generation deals with it. Do we have the tools and wherewithal to build new products and businesses? Or are we just trying to game our way into new dollars for ourselves. A new app? Maybe. A new platform? That might work, too. The entire American economy is propped up on the idea, as my son says, to "make a fuck ton of money." How is that going to be possible if we don't make and sell stuff? How do you make a fuck ton of money without irrational exuberance and excessive credit production? The entire economy has been handed over to the bankers and politicians. What do they care if we make stuff, or not?

The demise of the dollar and depreciation of the value of its physical aspect, i.e., the paper, has led to an obsession with accumulating wealth—greed!—without creating any value for anyone.

In past recoveries, industrial production always led the way to this idea of wealth; it was a dependable sign to measure the strength or weakness of the recovery. Production surged by an average of about 18% in the first two years after the typical recession. Since November 2001, though, when the so-called current economic expansion began, industrial production—the creation of goods and the traditional driver of the economy—has barely moved. In fact, the total number of factory jobs lost since the start of the most recent recession in March 2001 is 2.8 million. (We have lost a total of 3.4 million jobs since 1998.) This was the single greatest percentage fall in the labor force in almost eight decades since the Great Depression of the

1930s. What has been happening to American manufacturing can only be described with the word depression. And yet this important trend is almost invisible if we look at overall GDP.

This loss in the industrial base is not a temporary thing. It is a sharp downward plunge within a longer-term trend—going south and with the dollar's spending power soon to follow unless we turn it around. How does the loss of manufacturing jobs play into the true economic picture and, by association, the dollar crisis? Putting it another way, how is the news spun by the media?

In one headline on the topic in 2003, when the fallout from the 2001 recession was still being felt, we read: "Jobs: The Turning Point Is Here."[5] What was even more interesting in that story was a table titled "A Jobless Recovery? That Depends." Obviously, the author wanted to convey the message that the dismal employment picture was offset by good news elsewhere in the economy. But in fact, the story's statistics only confirmed that the US economy is in a wrenching crisis. Today a more timely news headline is "Making Less Than Dad," published on May 25, 2007, on CNN. The production side with high-paying jobs is disappearing, while the consumption side with low-paying jobs is booming. "There's a Job-Market Riddle at the Heart of the Next Recession," Bloomberg reads in 2022, and jobs are at the center again. "Tech giants and banks are already cutting workers," they continue, "but many employers seem desperate to keep hiring."

FICTITIOUS CAPITALISM, AGAIN

The gains in construction, commercial banking, and real estate were directly related to the housing and mortgage refinancing bubble. Look at the phenomenal growth in accommodation and services—10 times the numbers just a few years ago—and at temporary help services, which more than doubled.

What does such growth say about our real productivity? This employment record shows just how the economy's grossly distorted spending and growth pattern is moving. While the production side is collapsing, the consumption side is expanding.

Our economy is changing in big, big ways. We are moving away from goods production and toward services. It is a development that American policy makers and economists have hailed as a normal and natural shift in emphasis for a developed economy. This complacent view ignores two important points, though. First, the manufacturing sector pays the highest wages, which makes it a no-brainer for anyone to understand—especially anyone who has lost a manufacturing job and who now works in the retail sector. Second, manufacturing is the source of earnings that pay for the overseas obligations of every country. After a slight dip in 2005 to 53%, the United States is now at the point where our exports are at only 56% of our imports (57%, if you count the gold shipped out of the country). We know that manufacturing produces more and more goods while employing fewer and fewer people. But the American case is different; the production of goods increasingly lags behind growth in personal income. But so what? How does the balance of trade affect the typical American, and how does it hurt the dollar?

We read in our media that miraculous productivity gains have become the main driver of US GDP growth. But is this for real, or is it only a big economic hoax? We may hear a variety of possible explanations. For example, businesses are supposed to be able to squeeze more value out of the average worker. As this idea boosts profits, the impending comeback of business investment spending is taken for granted. The concept of improved productivity is supposed to offset lost market share in a global sense.

Labor productivity is an economic indicator that tells us how efficiently people work. In 2004—the year we supposedly put the recession behind us—labor productivity in business, which covers 70% of all labor productivity—sank to 2.9%. And in 2005 and 2006, the drop was really alarming: 2% and 1%, respectively. That will explain why the government jumped up and down about the surge in the third quarter of 2007. But keep in mind what I said earlier about surges. They imply that things are improving. This would be true if, at the same time, average wages were growing or at least keeping pace. The claim is contradicted by the numbers. The United States is going through an employment shift away from high-paying manufacturing jobs into low-paying jobs, in sectors like health services and retail.

If you want to make the hair on your head stand on end, check out the numbers from a recent survey by the Center on Budget and Policy Priorities, which studied data from the Commerce Department going back to 1929. In 2006, the share of national income that went to wages and salaries was the lowest on record. Since the 2001 recession, wages and salaries grew on average 1.9% annually, compared with corporate profits at 12.8%. In previous recoveries, wages and salaries grew at an average annual rate of 3.8%—that's nearly twice the recent rate—while corporate profits grew at 8.3%, about two-thirds the recent rate.

The belief that productivity growth is the whole deal is delusional, but as an economic principle, it is unique to American economists. In contrast, European economists rarely mentioned the notion. They know about the importance of productivity growth, but they view it as part of a more important trend, capital investment. American economists don't like to go there because it brings up the real problem with the relationship between employment and the value of the dollar. As a rule, where there is high capital investment, high productivity growth can also be taken for granted. And by the way, capital investment also provides the increase in demand and spending necessary to translate growing productivity into effectively higher employment and economic growth.

This concept—another no-brainer—is known to anyone who has studied history. The creation of jobs is part of the creation of infrastructure. In the United States of the nineteenth century, an era of building great railroads and canals created unprecedented economic growth and jobs. Those jobs were not created in the vacuum of a passive economy.

NICE WORK IF YOU CAN GET IT

So here we find ourselves, in the enigma of high productivity growth along with plunging employment. Why? Well, the American economists have the explanation, as always: High productivity growth goes hand in hand with jobless economic growth.

It's possible. But it might be worth pointing out that it has never happened before. It's a little like saying we can expect workers to work harder if we give them pay cuts. Higher productivity has always accompanied job creation, and that comes directly from capital investment. Old-fashioned productivity growth also involves genuine wealth creation through the building of factories and installation of machinery. The country's most recent productivity growth had nothing to do with capital investment, sadly.

There is only one logical explanation for this contrary indicator: It must have more statistical than economic causes. If we select economics, then we have to confront the facts: There is no reasonable economic explanation for the reported trend. The doubtful accuracy in reported productivity begins with the fact that real GDP growth is vastly overstated. This is due to inflation rates that have been systematically trimmed to the downside—falsified, if you will, to present a conclusion that is just not realistic. GDP is supposed to mean *growth* in the domestic economy. In practice, the numbers are not only inaccurate; they are misleading.

Around the world, inflation is based on measuring price changes. In the United States, we have moved away from that idea. Our economists prefer measuring consumer satisfaction or confidence. As a result, quality improvements and the so-called substitution effect play a key role in reducing reported inflation. Substitution refers to the way consumers alter their pattern of purchases as prices change. If beef prices rise, the consumer buys chicken. If air travel is too expensive, people drive or take a train or bus.

Our economic reporting system is like a vast national used car dealership, complete with fashion-challenged salespeople. We are being sold a lemon. The statistical gimmick of how inflation is reported, for example, means that our actual inflation rates are understated by around 2 percentage points per year, based on how the same trend is measured in other countries. The result: overstatement of GDP.

So inflation is higher than we think, and the GDP is not growing as well as we have been told. In assessing the value of our dollars on an after-tax and after-inflation basis, we are losing spending power. If we use the phony government inflation number, we are not even breaking even. This problem is not limited to how our savings and investment values are being eroded. It goes far beyond the cost of milk or tomatoes.

If we look at changes in business investment, what do we find?

According to conventional reports, a great rebound in business investment spending is already in full swing, primarily in the high-tech sector. But the so-called investment rebound comes completely from the way we price computers. You'd have to have a Ph.D. in "statistical economics" to understand the method used by the BEA to account for price declines in the computer industry brought on by natural competition for their products.

"The inflation-adjusted figure for investment in computers is no longer published," is the way the BEA describes it, "because [the US Department of] Commerce was concerned the rapid price declines for computers made the figures misleading."

Doesn't that statement seem odd? The reported rate of productivity growth comes from the potential production of computers, not from their actual use. But all the talk of the high productivity effects of computers logically relates to such effects from their use, of which we know nothing. Why? Because they are impossible to measure. The pricing of computers creates absurdly exaggerated perceptions of the money being spent and earned on computers—resulting in correspondingly higher GDP growth.

For example, under such a pricing scheme, computer producers reported an increase in revenue of $128.2 billion, or 49%, from $262.1 billion to $390.3 billion between first quarter 2002 and third quarter 2003. Very nice. *But* in actual dollars, the gain was only $16.4 billion, from $71.9 billion to $88.3 billion. BEA's inflated report created a boom for what was, in effect, a trickle. From an economic perspective, this contrast is huge, and the phony numbers are what most people use to draw conclusions.

Given the disparities between economic reporting and the real world, the economic importance of high-tech industries has been and continues to be overhyped in the United States. In terms of sales, employment, and earned profits, it is a sector of minor importance. The high-tech profit performance has been abysmal. Remember the industrial revolution and its lessons. Implementing new technologies involves radical changes across the economies, requiring and creating huge new industries with soaring employment. It radically changes economic and personal life. Is our so-called technological revolution a new industrial revolution? Hardly. By comparison, the new high-tech industries—what Andy Kessler refers to as the iPod Economy—are marginal. At the very least, measuring production based on these sectors is deceptive.

Under the official methodology—meaning reports from the government and from the official National Income and Product Accounts (NIPA)[6]— the profit picture is impressive. But a variety of profit studies tell a different story. Most economists have a great liking for the most comprehensive figure: corporate profits with inventory valuation and capital consumption adjustments. This is a fuzzy number. For one thing, it obscures what is really going on in the trend, as it includes the financial sector and now exceeds $1.6 trillion. Since their lows during the recessionary years, the aggregate numbers have grown by about 60%. But including the financial sector is a problem.

In what we may term the "real economy" (i.e., excluding the financial sector), the numbers are quite different. This nonfinancial real economy experienced pretax profits at a low of $357.2 billion in 2001 from a peak of $573.4 billion in 1997. Even with gradually increasing reported profits through 2006 (reaching $814.3 billion by the third quarter) the numbers remain, well, flat. This is true when we look at manufacturing alone, where we find that the numbers are no higher than they were in the previous decade. The gain for the nonfinancial sector has overwhelmingly come from retail trade, and we have to confront what this means in terms of jobs as well as profits. When we compare typical manufacturing profits and see a decade-long flat line, it is difficult to justify claims of an improved economy.

TIKTOK, TOILET PAPER, AND INFLATION PSYCHOSIS

The companies that were able to provide goods and services during the pandemic, while everyone was home, saw stark increases in S&P valuations. Everyone went online; everyone wanted to buy stuff without leaving their beds; people were in desperate need of entertainment—and toilet paper. Netflix, Amazon, Meta (then Facebook), and TikTok. The pandemic created an economic aberration we're all familiar with; one which, in late 2022, no one really knows what to make of yet. It's hard to build a business when you can't read the tea leaves while being forced to sit on your couch. We do want to make it exceptionally clear, however, that the inflation we are seeing today is not the result of coming out of our hidey-holes; rather, it is the result of the cheap money bailout extravaganza that happened from 2009–2018. The pandemic was just the icing on the cake.

This economic aberration in our reported GDP numbers—what politicians have generously called growth—is a bubble-driven spending surge. Initially, the emotional experience of the pandemic gave a boost to profits for S&P 500 companies as everyone was locked in and shopping online. Income-driven spending derives from wages and salaries, which—from another point of view—are also business expenses. In contrast, credit-financed spending increases business revenues.

Now we apply the same logic to what happens in the economy as a whole. Just as a corporation is limited in how far it can improve its bottom line, the consumer is also subject to economic laws. What turned cost cutting of the past few years into profits for businesses was a debt-driven economy. Consumers increased their spending despite heavy losses and funded it through higher borrowing.

CHAPTER 6

A MODERN ENIGMA

"I put a dollar in the change machine, nothing changed."

—George Carlin

It is a modern enigma. The US dollar—the world's reserve currency—is weakening, shrinking, falling at home. It has been since the inception of the Federal Reserve, the very institution assigned with the task of maintaining its value, but the decline has accelerated at an alarming rate of late. The popular term used for the demise of the dollar, by journalists and bloggers alike, is "inflation."

But here's the enigma. At the same time prices are rising for gas, eggs, and jeans, the US dollar is getting "stronger" against the euro, yen, and yuan—currencies from Europe, Japan, and China that make up the balance of trade in the global economy. How can that be?

How can the dollar be weakening at home and getting stronger in the global economy at the same time? The answer begins with an important distinction. We need to understand what it means to be a "reserve currency" of global commerce. And why that's different from what our friend and the author of the foreword to this book, Jim Rickards, calls a "payment currency." I'm going to write that again because it's important. For the balance of this book we'll need to understand the difference between a "reserve" and a "payment" currency. The distinction will also help us understand the historic inflation—price increases for everything—that began during the COVID-19 pandemic.

Fifteen years ago—the week we were putting the finishing touches on our second edition of *The Demise of the Dollar*—an early internet meme crossed my email inbox claiming that the world's prettiest face, Gisele Bündchen, wanted to be paid in euros for US modeling gigs. Around the same time, in a music video for his song "Blue Magic," the American rap artist Jay-Z triumphantly flashed multi-colored "yo-yos"—not dollars—in front of the camera. Black Friday that same year, anxious retailers opened their doors before dawn to let in crazed shoppers thirsty for bargains; it was mainly tourists from overseas who packed the streets of New York City that autumn, rabid and ready to shove their way to good deals. "I just saved $2,000 on this Rolex," flexed one shopper from the UK, waving her new wristwatch in a reporter's face like a fistful of dollars. The Canadians came bearing loonies too, which had reached parity with the US dollar in September 2007—for the first time since 1976. It was quite a time. And very different from now, writing this current and special third edition.

Today pretty faces, wealthy rappers, desperate US retailers, and happy Canadian shopaholics have finally brought about a financial reckoning day. What has changed since 2008? What changed helps us to tell the story of the dollar as a proxy of the world's most prominent currency.

TRIFFIN'S PARADOX

It's known as "Triffin's paradox" or "Triffin's dilemma." In the 1960s, Belgian-American economist Robert Triffin observed a paradox that arises when short-term domestic interests don't jive with long-term international objectives for a country like the United States whose currency serves as the "global reserve currency."

If foreign nations—France or Saudi Arabia, for example—want to hold the US dollar to buy US treasuries as a way to store wealth or use the US dollar or buy commodities like oil or gold priced in US dollars, the US Treasury has to be willing to supply the world with an extra supply of dollars. The printing presses whir and an excess of dollars get spit out to meet world demand.

More US dollars are not necessarily good for consumers or investors who use the currency for purchases and investments in their own economy. More dollars globally, also mean a weaker dollar at home. It is, as Triffin identified, a real dilemma.

So let's begin by defining the terms. A "reserve currency" is used to settle payments between nations, global banks, trading firms, and international corporations. When the Banque de France wants to settle payments for oil with the Kingdom of Saudi Arabia, they have historically used the US dollar as a medium of exchange because oil has historically been priced in US dollars. When the Hong-Kong Shanghai Banking Company (HSBC) wants to buy gold from the Swiss bank UBS, gold is priced in dollars. Using US dollars as a means for exchange globally is why it's considered a "reserve" currency. Nations, banks, and corporations use it to facilitate global trade.

During a global financial crisis—like those created by the meltdown of tech stocks in 2000–2001, the collapse of housing and financial panic of 2008–2009 or the greater inflation and supply chain shock caused by the COVID-19 pandemic lockdowns and the Russian invasion of Ukraine—investors try to sell their stocks and speculative assets to buy US Treasuries, gold or commodities. These latter assets are considered "safety trades," places to preserve your wealth. Well, guess what? Those assets are all priced in US dollars. So in order to get out of risky assets during a crisis, the "reserve" status of the dollar strengthens. Everybody wants the safety trades, but they have to buy dollars to get them. As a consequence the "dollar index" goes up. The index, or DXY if you want to trade it, measures the value of the dollar against a basket of other currencies including the euro and yen, but also includes the British pound, Swiss franc, Canadian dollar, and Swedish kroner. (Notably, the Chinese yuan has not been included to the index as of yet.) When the dollar index goes up, we call it a "strong dollar." That's great if you're an American living in Paris, as we were when the first edition of this book was written. We were earning money in dollars, but spending in euros; a strong dollar is like getting a raise without changing jobs or anything in your daily routine. A strong dollar is great if you never leave the United States.

Which brings us to the definition of a "payment currency." Those are the digits in your credit card or savings account you use to buy gas, clothes, cars, rent, mortgage, heat, and what have you. It's also the currency you use to buy all the ingredients of your cheeseburger— the bun, the beef, the cheese, the lettuce, tomato, and mayonnaise. During "inflation," the price for everything in terms of the "payment currency" goes up.

Recently, the mainstream media, too, shows that "the dollar index"—the index used to measure the US dollar in relation to other international currencies—is as strong as it has been since the turn of the millennium. How can that be if we're also having generationally high inflation rates?

Domestically, that means your money, the dollar doesn't buy as much. It means higher prices for gas and groceries. To the layman, this makes no sense. Shouldn't a strong dollar be good for the American consumer? How can the dollar be getting stronger at the same time that prices for gas and groceries are going up like a hot air balloon?

Inflation, Explored

Adjusted for inflation, the rapper known as "50 Cent," Curtis Jackson, should actually be called 0.75357 cent now. That's because $0.75357 in 2022 has the same purchasing power as $0.50 in 2003.

Further definitions are required. There are two types of inflation. The one most people pay attention to is what's known as "demand" or "demand-pull" inflation. Consumers want to buy a refrigerator or a new suit. They think, "Ah, prices are going up, so I better buy my fridge sooner rather than pay more later." When a whole economy of buyers is thinking this way, they "pull" demand forward. Demand goes up. Even if supply were steady, prices would go up because more people want what's already there. If "demand-pull" gets too out of hand, consumer psychology kicks in, and people buy at an even quicker pace, further increasing demand. Further increasing prices. If it's really bad, we call it "inflation psychosis," a sentiment divorced from reality. You think prices are going up so you spend your money faster.

The second form of inflation comes from the "supply" side. During the COVID-19 pandemic, for example, when entire economies were on lockdown, the supply of goods getting to store shelves was completely interrupted. Shut down. You had a bit of "inflation psychosis" because consumers were hoarding things like bottled water, paper towels, toilet paper, canned goods, and pasta.

The short bout with psychosis in early 2020 did end relatively quickly as the goods started to reappear on shelves. But the more extensive damage to the "supply chains," exacerbated by the war in Ukraine, were one of the root causes of the 40-year historic inflationary period that began mid-year in 2021. (The other, of course, was massive government spending, including direct payments to citizens straight from the US treasury. As shocking as it was for a student of economics when the "stimmies"—economic stimulation checks—were first being distributed, we'll take up that situation in a later chapter.)

Back to "supply" side inflation. You may recall reports of cargo ships waiting off the coast of Long Beach, California, one of the nation's largest and most important sources of imports from China. The ships were waiting to dock and unload, but there were bottlenecks and not enough dockworkers to unload the shipping containers. The shipping containers were not getting loaded onto cargo trains or fed into the nation's extensive trucking system. And so on. Consumer demand remained high, but supply itself was blocked. The initial cause were the lockdowns themselves. But in the years following, opening the economy back up, well it's not as easy as flipping a switch. The "supply chains"—the many varied and different businesses, legal contracts, bills of lading, and regulatory practices, not to mention skill and talent of workers—all need to be rebuilt. With supply blocked and demand still high, you get "supply" side inflation. The price for goods and services go up, up and up. If supply for goods and services remain blocked for too long, inflation tips over from a logistical nightmare to a psychological one.

So, let's back up for a second. The modern enigma we began with is that the US dollar is both a "reserve currency" and a "payment currency." The dollar is a vital tool in the global banking system during a financial crisis. But it can also be suffering massive demise at home for those who use it during everyday transactions. The dollar can be strengthening at the same time that is worth less to you. How did this happen?

The dollar has mysteriously grown to new highs against other currencies. When currencies fluctuate against one another, the money in your wallet also fluctuates. We recall 2000 to 2004, we scribbled out our financial insights from an office in Paris. During one 18-month period beginning in late 2002, the cost of living for those expats among us—who were paid in dollars but spent money in euros—saw their cost of living go up by almost half. In 2007, it still cost about 50% more to live or travel in Western Europe. The day before Thanksgiving 2007, the dollar fell to $1.4856 per euro—its weakest rate of exchange since the euro debuted in 1999—but it's worse for *Daily Reckoning* colleagues who worked and or traveled to London (come on England!).

In 2022, the story would be entirely different. The dollar euro exchange rate had dropped to $0.94. . . less than a buck. It would be a good time to live in France and get paid in dollars again. That being said, the strong dollar diminishes the earnings of American companies selling goods overseas. And we'll see that quickly in their earnings reports, and further reflected in their stock prices. This is the beginning of the recession, on the back of a "strong dollar."

Recall: The dollar is only strong because it is used as a medium of exchange during a crisis. If you are an American salesman in Europe and are trying to price out your products and get a deal done, a strong dollar doesn't help because it makes people who aren't American less likely to engage in trade. A normal person's reaction to a strong dollar would be: "Aw sweet, let's go to Portugal and buy some Gucci." But that is not the economic reality. It might be good (and fun) for the moment, but in the long run your Gucci flip flops are more expensive than you think they are.

A MODERN DILEMMA IN YOUR BANK ACCOUNT

The Great Dollar Standard Era is a direct result of the removal of gold as the underpinning of the world's currencies. The vast overprinting of currency will inevitably debase the value of the US dollar, and because so many foreign currencies are pegged to the dollar, the currency of those nations as well. Fiat money, simply put, is created out of nothing. A future promise to pay has never supported monetary value for long, and the United States is so overextended today that it is doubtful it could ever honor its overall real debts. Counting obligations under Medicare and Social Security, the real debt of the United States is now approaching six times the reported national debt, estimates David Walker, former head of the Government Accountability Office (GAO), now president and chief executive officer of the newly founded Peter G. Peterson Foundation:

> Federal debt managed by the bureau [Bureau of the Public Debt] totaled about $9 billion at the end of fiscal year 2007. However, that number excludes many items, including the gap between scheduled and funded Social Security and Medicare benefits, veterans' health care, and a range of other commitments and contingencies that the federal government has pledged to support. If these items are factored in, the total burden in present federal dollars is estimated to be about $53 trillion. Stated differently, the estimated current total burden for every American is nearly $175,000; and every day that burden becomes larger.[1]

The argument favoring the current fiat system is that the demand for it grew out of barter, the need to facilitate ever-higher volumes of trade. If this were true, there would be a reasonable expectation that a system of paper drafts would make sense. But the reality is that fiat money has not grown out of barter, but from the previous gold standard. Given the lack of control over how much fiat money is placed in circulation—after all, it is based on nothing—we can only expect that the currency will continue to lose value over time. The model of fiat money is supported and defended with arguments that consumption is good for the economy, even with the use of vacant monetary systems. But there is a problem:

> The predictions of these models are at odds with the historical evidence. Fiat money did not in fact evolve . . . by means of a great leap forward from barter. Nor did fiat monies ever emerge out of thin air. Instead, fiat monies have always developed out of some previously existing money.[2]

Can we equate the problems inherent in fiat money with the effects of inflation? We have all heard that saving for retirement today is problematic because by the time we retire we will need more dollars to pay for the things we will need. By definition, this sounds like the consequences of inflation. But inflation is not simply higher prices; it has another aspect, which is devalued currency. We have to pay higher prices in the future because the currency is worth less relative to other currencies. That is the real inflation. Higher prices are only symptoms following the debasement of currency. If we examine *why* those prices go up, we discover that the reason is not necessarily corporate greed, inefficiency, or foreign price gouging. At the end of the day, it is the gradual loss of purchasing power, the need for more dollars to buy the same things. That's inflation. And fiat money is at the root of the problem.

The intrinsic problem with fiat money systems is how it unravels the basic economic reality. We know that it requires work to create real wealth. We labor and we are paid. We save and we earn interest. Government, however, produces nothing to create wealth, so it creates wealth out of an arbitrary system: fiat money. The problem is described well in the following passage:

> It takes work to create wealth. "Dollars" are created without any work—how much more work is involved in printing a $100 bill as compared to a $1 bill? Not only are ordinary people at home being deceived, but foreigners who accept and save our "dollars" in exchange for their goods and services are also being cheated.[3]

So are we "cheated" by the fiat money system? Under one interpretation, we have to contend with the reality that the dollar is not backed by anything of value. But as long as we all agree to assign value to the dollar, and as long as foreign central banks do the same, isn't it okay to use a fiat money system?

The problem becomes severe when, unavoidably, the system finally collapses. At some point, the Federal Reserve—with blessings of the Congress and the administration—prints and places so much money into circulation that its perceived value just evaporates. Can this happen? It has always happened in the past when fiat money systems were put into use. We have to wonder whether FDR was sincere when, in 1933, he declared that the currency had adequate backing. It wasn't until the following year that the president raised the ounce value of gold from \$20.67 to \$35. He explained his own monetary policy in 1933 after declaring the government's sole right to possess gold:

> More liberal provision has been made for banks to borrow on these assets at the Reserve Banks and more liberal provision has also been made for issuing currency on the security of those good assets. This currency is not fiat currency. It is issued on adequate security, and every good bank has an abundance of such security.[4]

It was the plan of the day. First, the law required that all citizens turn over their gold to the government. Second, the value of that gold was raised nearly 70% to \$35 per ounce (after collecting it from the people, of course). Third, the president declared that currency printing was being liberalized—but it is backed by gold, so it's not a fiat system. This may have been true in 1933, but since then—having removed ourselves from the gold standard—the presses are printing money late into the night. The gold standard has been long forgotten in Congress, the Federal Reserve, and the executive branch.

THE POLITICS OF THE ECONOMY

It may be the view of some people that a perfect monetary system may include changes in value based on purchasing power and on the demand for money itself. Thus, rich nations would become richer and control the cost of goods, while poor nations would remain poor. In spite of the best efforts under the Bretton Woods Agreement, it has proven impossible to simply let money find its own level of value. Unlike stocks and real estate, the free market does not work well with monetary value because each country has its own self-interests. Furthermore, today's post–Bretton Woods monetary system has no method available to prevent or mitigate trade imbalances. Thus, trade surplus versus deficit continues to expand out of control.

The United States ended up accumulating current account deficits totaling more than $3 trillion between 1980 and 2000. This perverse twist on world money has had a strange effect:

> These deficits have acted as an economic subsidy to the rest of the world, but they have also flooded the world with dollars, which have replaced gold as the new international reserve asset. These deficits have, in effect, become the font of a new global money supply.[5]

This is what occurs when international money supplies become unregulated. We need a firmly controlled world banking system if only to stop the unending printing of money. If, indeed, US deficits continue as a form of subsidy to the rest of the world, that can only lead to a worldwide economic collapse like the one seen in the 1920s and 1930s.

If it were possible to create a controlled international monetary unit, its effectiveness would demand ongoing regulation to prevent the disparities among nations with varying resources and reserves. Ludwig von Mises, noted twentieth-century economist, wrote:

> The idea of a money with an exchange value that is not subject to variations due to changes in the ratio between the supply of money and the need for it . . . demands the intervention of a regulatory authority in the determination of the value of money; and its continued intervention.[6]

Mises concluded that this need for intervention was itself a problem. It is unlikely that any governments would be trustworthy enough to properly ensure a *fair* valuation of money, were it left up to them; instead, governments are more likely than not to fall into the common fiat trap. Without limitations on how much money can be printed, it is human and governmental nature to print as much as possible. Mises observed that fiat money leads to monetary policy designed to achieve political aims:

> The state should at least refrain from exerting any sort of influence on the value of money. A metallic money, the augmentation or diminution of the quantity of metal available which is independent of deliberate human intervention, is becoming the modern monetary ideal.[7]

To an extent, the enactment of a fiat money system is likely either to be politically motivated or to soon become a political tool in the hands of government. We have to see how government attempts to influence economic health through a variety of means and in tandem with Federal Reserve policy: raising and lowering interest rates, enacting tax incentives for certain groups, legislating tax cuts or tax increases, and imposing or reducing trade restrictions or tariffs. All of these moves invariably have a pro and con argued politically rather than economically. The argument in modern-day US politics is between Republican desires to reduce taxes as a means of stimulating growth versus Democratic views that we cannot afford tax cuts and such cuts are given to favored upper-income taxpayers. The arguments are complex and endless, but they are not just political tools; they are part of overall monetary and economic policy trends as well.

This has become our modern entry in the history of money. The belief on the part of government, rooted in an arrogant thinking that *power* extends even to the valuation of goods and services and monetary exchange, has led to a monetary policy that makes utterly no sense in historical perspective. Having gone over entirely to a fiat standard, government has chosen to ignore history and those market forces that ultimately decide the question of valuation, in spite of anything government does. This has always been true, as Jeffrey M. Herbener observed:

> The use of the precious metals was historically the choice of the market. Without interference from governments, traders adopted the parallel standard using gold and silver as money.[8]

If monetary policy were left alone and allowed to function in the free market, what would happen? Perhaps governments ultimately do follow the market by adopting the gold standard, as we have seen repeatedly in history: going on the gold standard, moving to fiat money, experiencing a debasement, and then returning to the gold standard. Herbener continued by observing:

> The fly in the ointment of the classical gold standard was precisely that since it was created and maintained by governments, it could be abandoned and destroyed by them. As the ideological tide turned against laissez-faire in favor of statism, governments intent upon

expanding the scope of their interference in and control of the market economy found it necessary to eliminate the gold standard.[9]

Today, we live with that legacy. While historians marvel at the "end of history" and the triumph of free market economics, the Fed maintains "price controls" on the very symbol of economic freedom—the US dollar itself.

Would letting someone else be the financial policeman (and everything that comes with that) of the world be the worst thing? What happened to the idea that you can just live independently and do your own thing? You can't even do that with your own money anymore.

CHAPTER 7

SHORT, UNHAPPY
EPISODES
IN MONETARY
HISTORY

History is a vast early warning system.

—Norman Cousins

People have been fighting over the value of money since. . . forever.
The whole basis for money itself—currency as a means of commerce—is based on tangible value. In other words, money is not the
greenbacks we carry around; it is supposed to be the gold or other
metal backing it up. The dollar is a promissory note. Check what it
says at the top of the bill itself: "Federal Reserve Note."

Today, the American dollars in circulation are just a bunch of IOUs.
That would be fine if the gold reserves were sitting in Fort Knox to
back up those IOUs . . . but they are not. The Fed just keeps printing
more and more money, and it will eventually catch up with us. The day
will come when we will have to pay off those IOUs, not only domestically but to foreign investors too.

History has shown that money—not counterfeit, but *official*
money printed by the government—has been known to lose value

and become virtually worthless. Examples include Russian rubles from pre-Revolution days, 50-million marks from 1920s Germany, and Cuban pesos from pre-Castro days. In all of these cases, jarring political and economic change destroyed currency values—suddenly, completely, and permanently.

What kinds of events could do the same thing to the US dollar, and what can you do today to position yourself strategically? The potential fall of the dollar is good news if you know what steps to take today. We're not as insulated as many Americans believe. In the 1930s, 20% of all US banks went broke, and 15% of life savings went up in smoke. After the emergency measures put into effect by President Franklin D. Roosevelt through the Emergency Banking Relief Act of 1933, confidence was restored with another piece of legislation: the 1933 Glass-Steagall Act. This bill created the Federal Deposit Insurance Corporation (FDIC), insuring all US bank deposits against loss.

The severity of the growing situation had been seen well in advance. The financial newspaper *Barron's,* established in 1921, editorialized in 1933:

> Since early December, Washington had known that a major banking and financial crisis was probably inevitable. It was merely a question of where the first break would come and the manner of its coming.[1]

Two weeks earlier, the same column cautioned its readers that when the dollar begins to lose value, this leads to a series of "flights"—from property into bank deposits, then from deposits into currency, and finally from currency into gold.[2]

We can apply these astute observations from 1933 to today's currency situation. The government, anticipating a flight from currency into gold, had already made hoarding gold or even owning it illegal. The second step—insuring accounts in federal banks—helped to calm down the mood. By preventing the panic, these actions enabled the currency to be stabilized. But in those times, we were still on the gold standard. The currency in circulation was, in fact, backed by something. Remember, that riverboat gambler who keeps asking for ever-higher markers will eventually run out of credit. At some point the casino boss will realize that the gambler's ability to repay is questionable. Maybe those markers are just a heap of IOUs that can never be cashed in.

In the 1930s, the causes of the Great Depression were complex but related to a series of obvious abuses in monetary, financial, and banking policies. History has simplified the issue by blaming the Depression on the stock market crash. The stock market crash, one of many symptoms of policies run amok, has lessons for modern times. The unbridled printing of money—expansion of the IOU economy—is good news for those who recognize the potential for gold.

We hear experts on TV and in the print media shrugging off the deficit problems. "Our economy is strong and getting stronger" is the mantra of those with a vested interest in keeping dollars flowing: Wall Street brokers and analysts, for example. But we cannot ignore the facts. The federal deficit is growing by more than $40 billion per month. It is *not* realistic to point to this economy and say it's doing just fine.

Gold is the beneficiary of reckless monetary policies *and* the political expedience of the War on Terror, the Financial Panic of '08, and the COVID-19 pandemic lockdowns. But there's more to the story.

The average value of an ounce of gold over the first two decades of the twenty-first century has been a relatively consistent story. From the 1999 low of $253, the gold price went on a decade-long tear. By February 2012, in the post-Panic of '08 bailout period, gold topped out $2,308—a decade long gain of 882%.

Over the ensuing decade it never dropped below $1,300 only to retest the 2012 high in the middle of the COVID pandemic lockdowns. In August of 2020, gold was back at $2,250. (See Figure 7.1.)

The cause of this change in gold's price may be attributed to the political response to the attack on the World Trade Center, the mortgaged-back securities, and the debacle of government pandemic policies. It reflects equally on the Fed's monetary policies and debt-based economic recovery. During the same period that gold prices have begun to rise, we should also take a look at the trend in money in circulation. We have to look at the price movement as an overreaction to the whole gold-to-currency relationship.

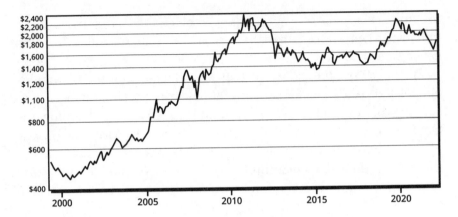

FIGURE 7.1 Gold Price, 1999–2022

Source: macrotrends.net

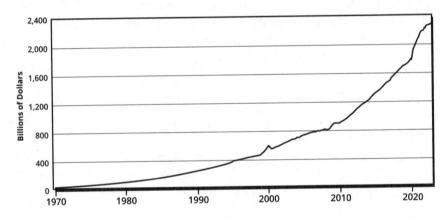

FIGURE 7.2 US Currency in Circulation, 1971–2022

Source: Federal Reserve.

The sheer amount of US dollars is troubling for the dollar itself, but—again—great news for gold. Remember what the world economic and political situation was like in the early 1970s: a weakening dollar, easy money, and international unrest. Sound familiar? We're back in the same combination of circumstances that were present when gold prices went from $35 to more than $850 per ounce in 1980. Since 1995, the value of currency in circulation has nearly doubled (up 95.7%); by 2006, the "phony money" pumped into the economy reached $783.5 billion. The Fed's policy sounds like a replay of that popular milk commercial: "Need money? We'll print more."

The numbers prove that gold is going to be the investment of the future. World mining in gold averages 80 million ounces per year, but demand has been running at 110 million ounces. So if central banks want to hold the value of gold steady, at least 30 million ounces per year must be sold into the market. This creates a squeeze. As the dollar weakens, central banks will want to increase their holdings in gold bullion, not sell it off. This is why gold's price has started to rise and must continue to rise into the future. As long as that demand grows—and it will rise as the dollar's value continues falling—the price of gold simply has to reflect the forces of supply and demand.

But, you might ask, why do central banks want to hold down the value of gold? We have to recognize how this whole money game works. Most world currencies are off the gold standard, following the US example. So as gold's value rises, it competes with each country's currency. Of course, the trend toward weakening currencies and the continuing demand for gold mean that the growth in gold's value could continue strongly for many years to come.

SMOKE AND MIRRORS

When the United States removed its currency from the gold standard, it seemed to make economic sense at the time. President Nixon saw this as the solution to a range of economic problems and, combined with wage and price freezes, printing as much money as desired looked like a good idea. Unfortunately, most of the world's currencies followed suit. The world economy now runs primarily on a fiat money system.

Fiat money is so-called because it is not backed by any tangible asset such as gold, silver, or even seashells. The issuing government has decreed by fiat that "this money is a legal exchange medium, and it is worth what we say." So, lacking a gold backing or backing of some other precious metal, what gives the currency value? Is there a special reserve somewhere? No. Some economists have tried to explain away the problems of fiat money by pointing to the vast wealth of the United States in terms of productivity, natural resources, and land. But even if those assets are counted, they're not liquid. They're not part of the system of exchange. We have to deal with the fact that fiat money holds its value only as long as the people using that money continue to believe it has value—and as long as they continue to find people who will accept the currency in exchange for goods and services. The value of fiat money relies on confidence and expectation. So as we continue to increase twin deficit bubbles and as long as consumer debt keeps rising, our fiat money will eventually lose value. Gold, in comparison, has tangible value based on real market forces of supply and demand.

The short-term effect of converting from the gold standard to fiat money has been widespread prosperity. So the overall impression is that US monetary policy has created and sustained this prosperity. Why abandon the dollar when times are so good?

This is where the great monetary trap is found. If we study the many economic bubbles in effect today, we know we eventually have to face up to the excesses and that a big correction will occur. That means the dollar will fall, and gold's value will rise as a direct result.

The sad lesson of economic history will be that when the gold standard is abandoned and governments can print too much money, they will. That tendency is a disaster for any economic system because excess money in circulation (too much debt, in other words) only encourages consumer behavior mirroring that policy. Thus, we find ourselves in record-high levels of credit card debt, refinanced mortgages, and personal bankruptcies—all connected to that supposed prosperity based on printing far too much currency: the fiat system.

We can see where this overprinting will lead. As debt grows relative to GDP, we would expect to see positive signs elsewhere, such as growth in new jobs. But like a Tiananmen Square Rolex watch deal, the value simply isn't there. There is some job growth, but in reality, there is also a decline in earnings. High-paying manufacturing jobs have been replaced and exceeded by low-paying retail and health care sector jobs, so even if more people are at work, real earnings are down. Instead of simply measuring the number of jobs, an honest tracking system would also compare average wages and salaries in those jobs. Then we would be able to see what is really going on— more low-paying jobs being created, replacing high-paying jobs being lost.

THE NEW ROMAN EMPIRE

In 20 BC, the Roman Emperor Augustus began printing money faster than gold production, even though he'd ordered gold mines to produce 24 hours per day in the outlying regions of the Empire. Future emperors followed the pattern, spending nonstop. Nero reduced the currency's value intentionally in order to continue spending, and ever-larger trade deficits resulted between Rome and its colonies and trading partners. Of course, these policies were part of the larger gradual decline of the Roman Empire.

History provides many examples along these lines. About 1,100 years ago, China issued paper money but eventually abandoned the practice because excessive currency in circulation caused inflation. When Spain found gold in Mexico in the sixteenth century, it became the world's richest nation. The Spanish used the gold to buy, buy, buy, and to expand their military influence. But the wars eventually used up their wealth, so Spain began issuing debt to pay the bills, leading of course to loss of its economic and military power. The French went through a similar period in the eighteenth century, printing way too much paper money and suffering unbelievable levels of inflation as a consequence.

President Abraham Lincoln authorized the use of paper currency with the Legal Tender Act. The result, once again, was runaway inflation. The debt financed the Civil War, but it created a widespread disdain for the practice, at least until 1913 when the Federal Reserve was created.

In the twentieth century, we saw many examples of monetary disasters. In Germany during the 1920s, war reparations destroyed the economy and large amounts of paper money were printed in an attempt to pay reparations (paying imposed debt with new debt). Of course, it didn't achieve anything but massive devaluation. In 1934, the United States joined the trend. Roosevelt set the value of gold at $35 per ounce in an attempt to end the Great Depression. And we know that, years later, Presidents Nixon and Ford completed the cycle of removal from the gold standard once and for all.

The effect has been worldwide, and it only makes the case for investing in gold more compelling. We see repeatedly from history that when countries are on the gold standard, they thrive—and when they go off the gold standard, that move leads to trouble. The problems seem to appear after 30 years. So if we count from the Nixon decision of 1971 to go off the gold standard, we should have seen problems soon after 2001. It was in 2002, in fact, when the value of gold started its current rise. So the 30 years of prosperity after removal of the gold standard have come to an end.

FIAT MONEY SYSTEMS OF THE PAST

A short trek along the dusty crossroads of history is all it takes to see that time and again when countries go off the gold standard, trouble ensues. The gold standard forces spending discipline on politicians, despots, demagogues, and democrats. When a country is on the gold standard, it has to live within its means. But when it goes off the gold standard and begins using fiat money, the sky's the limit.

That's when the trouble begins.

As long as a government—any government—is able to print money indefinitely, you can bet that it will. A government cannot be trusted to control its spending ways any more than a college freshman with dad's unlimited credit card during spring break. If the temptation is put out there, governments are going to go too far. Unfortunately, even the best economic experts can only identify when the printing of money has gone too far by one yardstick: when the system implodes. By then it's too late to prevent the damage.

Let's review some ill-fated historical examples.

The Roman Empire—In 20 BC, Augustus ordered Gallic mines to operate around the clock to fund ever-growing infrastructure costs. Even so, the Empire continued printing money beyond its reserves, causing inflation. The trend was followed by subsequent emperors until 64 AD, when the infamous Nero cut back on the amount of silver in coins. Poor monetary policy coupled with abuses among the elite led to the eventual fall of the entire Empire.

China, Ninth Century AD—A new innovation, paper money, came into being. It was described as "flying money" because a breeze could blow it out of a holder's hand. Originally meant as a temporary fix for a copper shortage, the paper money system got out of control. As one might predict, it was all too easy to just keep printing, which led to uncontrolled inflation. As bad an idea as it was, Marco Polo took some paper money back with him to Europe, where few people believed his tall tales of Chinese paper money. He described how seriously the Chinese took their paper money when he wrote:

> All these pieces of paper are issued with as much solemnity and authority as if they were pure gold or silver; and on every piece a variety of officials, whose duty it is, have to write their names, and to put their seals. And when all is duly prepared, the chief officer deputed by the Khan smears the Seal entrusted to him with vermilion, and impresses it on the paper, so that the form of the Seal remains printed upon it in red: the Money is then authentic. Anyone forging it would be punished with death.[3]

A few hundred years later, the Europeans were ready to take a shot at making their own solemn version of paper money.

Spain, Fifteenth Century—Spain grew to become the richest country in the world, based primarily on gold discoveries in Mexico. Spain, a country of contradictions, enjoyed growing wealth while running the infamous Spanish Inquisition, one of its darker moments. In 1481, Ferdinand and Isabella appointed the notorious inquisitor Tomás de Torquemada to run the show. So the availability of wealth led to colonial adventurism, social cruelty, and eventually excessive debt and national bankruptcy.

France, Eighteenth Century—John Law tried to revolutionize money and the way it was used. He said, "My secret is to make gold out of paper."[4] This early Western experiment with paper money has formed the basis of today's widespread currency systems. France, suffering from the abuses of the court of Louis XIV, had a nearly worthless coinage system. The king, during the last 14 years of his rule, spent two billion livres above tax collections. Law's idea to fix the problem was to create notes (paper money) to facilitate trade. By 1717, Law had put an elaborate Ponzi scheme into play. He promised riches to anyone who invested in his private bank. The government granted him exclusive rights to control the currency, print money, control sea trade, and administer revenues from tobacco, salt, and the exaggerated riches of France's newest colony, Louisiana. Speculation accelerated and, by 1720, the scheme began falling apart. Before it was over, the paper money lost 90% of its face value. Law died in 1729 and an epitaph was published that year in France: "Here lies that celebrated Scotsman, that peerless mathematician who, by the rules of algebra, sent France to the poorhouse."[5]

United States, Eighteenth Century—By 1764, the United States was plagued by a volume of worthless notes. Issued during the French and Indian War, these notes brought about a widespread economic recession. Britain declared that the Colonies were no longer allowed to issue drafts or paper money. During the Revolutionary War, Congress authorized paper money to be printed. This so-called continental money was supposed to be backed by gold and silver, and each state promised to provide a share of bullion reserves as collateral. But it never happened and, predictably, continental money was printed with no backing. Making matters worse, the British subverted the effort by counterfeiting their own version of the bills. The money became worthless, and by 1780, anything of little value was described as being "not worth a continental."[6] Finally, in 1781, continentals could be redeemed for newly issued Treasury notes. The new superintendent of finance, Robert Morris, issued these, and they became known as "Morris notes." They were redeemable in hard currency at a date noted on the bills, but, lacking any real reserves, these notes also declined in value.[7]

France, Eighteenth Century, Part II—France had been deceived by John Law and his currency magic but didn't learn from the lesson. By 1791, France was ready to try paper currency again. The government, in anti-aristocracy mode, confiscated property and other assets from the wealthy in exchange for *assignats,* notes that paid interest, operating like land mortgage notes. Far from solving the problem of economic disparity among the classes, the extreme measures only made matters worse. Within four years, inflation had risen by 13,000%. Few instruments have declined to zero value as quickly as the *assignats.* In a foreword to a book on the historical implications of French monetary policy, John Mackay described France's attempts at a fiat money system as

> the most gigantic attempt ever made in the history of the world
> by a government to create an inconvertible paper currency, and to

maintain its circulation at various levels of value. It also records what is perhaps the greatest of all government efforts . . . to enact and enforce a legal limit of commodity prices. Every fetter that could hinder the will or thwart the wisdom of democracy had been shattered. . . . But the attempts failed. They left behind them a legacy of moral and material desolation and woe.[8]

A NEW SHAYS' REBELLION?

In January 1787, Daniel Shays, a former officer in the Revolutionary Army, led 2,000 farmers in a revolt against US government troops at a Springfield, Massachusetts, armory. The rebels, mostly farmers, were protesting serious economic conditions, the worst of which was the lack of a stable currency. They demanded that the government create what they called "sound money." In other words, the farmers were demanding a gold-backed dollar. There was a lot of money in circulation, but very little of it was worth its face value.

The 2,000 rebels were arrested and the leaders were given death sentences, but all were later pardoned. This was an early and relatively small example of what can happen when a country does not have sound money.

The farmers who followed Daniel Shays knew that their economic survival depended on fixing the problem. Their actions forced the government to create a single currency and control it. Now, more than 200 years later, we face a similar problem but on a far larger scale. Physical rebellion is not the solution today, but many serious problems remain: unfair and inconsistent taxation, expensive lawsuits, and excessively high salaries for government cronies. Sound familiar? These were among the complaints that led to Shays' Rebellion.

Argentina, Nineteenth and Twentieth Centuries—Perhaps learning from the mistakes of the Europeans, Argentina went on the gold standard in 1853. For the next century, the economy thrived. In 1943, Juan Peron's coup destroyed the country's system, and the gold reserves disappeared, to be replaced by paper money. This began a downward-spiraling economy that has only recently begun to recover.

United States, Nineteenth Century—During the Civil War, President Lincoln authorized issuance of paper money to help finance the war effort. The resulting inflation caused a public sentiment against paper money that lasted until 1913, when the Federal Reserve System was devised.

Germany, Twentieth Century—In 1923, the so-called Weimar Republic—a post–World War I temporary government—had to deal with repressive war reparations. It began printing massive amounts of paper money to make payments, to the extent that the currency became completely worthless. The devastation paved the way for the Nazi movement of the late 1920s and early 1930s, and directly to World War II.

United States, Twentieth Century—The United States has removed itself from the gold standard in the most recent switch to a fiat money system. This took place in three phases. First, in 1934, President Roosevelt declared that an ounce of gold was to be valued at $35, up from its previous level of $20.67. The hope was that this change would end the Depression. Second, the Bretton Woods system agreed upon in 1944 (explained at the beginning of this book) achieved worldwide agreement to peg currencies to gold. But in practice, the US dollar became an international currency and other countries pegged their currencies to the dollar. Bretton Woods also opened the door to widespread use of debt (i.e., printing of additional currency above gold reserves) to facilitate international trade. Third, in 1971, President Nixon ended convertibility of dollars to gold. The United States had already been printing paper money far above reserve levels; this removal from the gold standard destroyed the Bretton Woods Agreement, creating a worldwide gold drain.

THE GREAT DOLLAR STANDARD ERA

The fiat money system in effect in the United States today makes this point. It may be interesting to note that today many economists fear that a *return* to the gold standard or institution of an international monetary system could actually trigger a depression—a collapse of the financial economy. One author made an attempt to tie the Great Depression to England's attempt to return to the gold standard in the

1920s.[9] However, most historians would agree that trying to go back to the gold standard was not actually the cause of the worldwide depression. The cause was more likely out-of-control credit resulting from suspension of the gold standard. The global economy was in trouble at least a full decade prior to England's change in monetary policy.

However, the book made a good point: It is no simple matter to revert to a more sensible standard. Consequences are inevitable. It would not be easy for the major currencies to return to an organized Bretton Woods Agreement type of system. Growth has occurred at such an accelerated pace that an attempt to return to the gold standard in one move would not work. This does not mean that the fiat money system can succeed. To the contrary, no such system has in the past.

No fiat money system has ever succeeded. History has shown time and again that eventually excessive government spending makes paper money worthless. Today, the common belief among US economists and the Federal Reserve is that consumption is the fix-all. The fact that consumption is taking place with borrowed money does not seem to matter. So consumer debt, national budget deficits, and trade gaps have become a sort of norm, whereas in the past all of these economic trends were viewed as early warning signs of a weakening currency.

An argument against the gold standard is based on gold's rarity. We cannot expect any economic expansion as long as we are held back by a commodity in limited supply, the argument goes. However, the argument is flawed.

Supply and demand alter the value of every commodity in an efficient economic system. As demand increases for a unit of exchange (i.e., gold), the price rises. This is an efficient system. Demand pushes the price up, and supply pushes the price down. When paper money is in use, the whole efficiency of the economic system goes out the window. As long as the government can print more money, it can continue to expand a consumption base in spite of any supply and demand, and in spite of the limited supply of gold itself.

Eventually, though, all of that printed money exceeds its own life cycle. It becomes worthless, as we have seen time and again—in Rome, China, Spain, France, Germany, and now the United States.

Perhaps a paper money system pegged specifically to commodity reserves would give the currency the stability it needs and rein in government spending. We don't pretend to know the solution to a runaway fiat regime. But experience tells us that governments have less discipline than a hungry fat man at an all-you-can-eat buffet. They are simply going to print, print, print, until the system fails. Is this a matter of weak character or simply human nature? Some, like Clif Droke, have argued that governments "must be composed of men of the highest moral standing, and ideally should be Christian in composition."[10] Who is going to decide what constitutes the highest morals, and what track record gives Christians a monopoly on integrity?

The monetary system is evolving before our very eyes. Never before in human history has the reserve currency of the world been so burdened with debt. And never has the transfer of one international currency to another been peaceful. Is the euro likely to supplant the dollar as international money?[11] Perhaps it will be the Chinese yuan.

During debate on the Bretton Woods Agreement, John Maynard Keynes hinted at the desirability of a world central banking system and a world currency. We have not had such a system since the sixth century, when the Roman coin the solidus (originally minted by Emperor Constantine) was "accepted everywhere from end to end of the earth."[12] The solidus was respected for centuries, while it also competed with the dinar in the Moslem world. Both coins held their value for good reason: The metallic content of these coins remained consistent over time, and robust economic activity spread their use throughout the known world.

Both coins lost value in about the nineteenth century, and for the same reason: reduction of metallic weight. In an effort to stretch currency values, rulers reduced weight, causing debasement and, eventually, loss of trust in the market. The introduction of inferior-grade coins further accelerated the debasement of the traditional solidus and dinar.[13]

The next go-round of worldwide coinage occurred in the thirteenth century. In Italy, the *genoin* (introduced in Genoa) and the *florin* (from Florence) became true world currencies during a period of expanding international trade. Two hundred years later, the system expanded with introduction of the *ducato* in Venice.[14]

These coins held steady in value until the fifteenth century, when silver mining in several European countries changed valuation of metals. It is interesting to note that debasement of these currencies was not accompanied by inflation. This was due to the fact that as money supplies grew, so did real output and production. By today's standards, it was a minuscule economy, but the model made the point concerning valuation of currency-based monetary systems and their relationship with production and consumption.

The characteristics that made older international monetary systems stable included high unitary value; intrinsic stability; and strong economic trade, production, and balance of consumption.[15] A fourth attribute is widespread acceptance of a currency as a means of acceptable monetary value.

In comparison to modern fiat money systems, these attributes become significant. We can judge the actual health of a monetary system by comparing its attributes to these older international systems. An argument made by US economists and the chairman of the Federal Reserve is that the United States does, indeed, enjoy all of those attributes in its monetary system. But the various consumption bubbles that control the US economy belie this opinion. In fact, we may be on the verge of seeing the dollar being replaced gradually by another medium, perhaps the euro. The study of history has shown:

> A series of international monies has existed historically, each occupying center stage sometimes for several centuries and eventually being replaced by the next. The only exception is the dollar, which is the current international money and, therefore, has not been replaced. . . . The euro area is large enough in terms of trade to be a serious competitor to the dollar as an international money.[16]

"The solution, ultimately, to the problem of governmental abuse of its printing presses is to establish a modern-day international currency." I wrote those words before Bitcoin came out of anyone's mouth. We're still looking for that solution. But is there a solution at all? Won't it always be this way. Perhaps, like all things, the best approach to the greenback boogie is moderation, though that requires a complex understanding of the cycles which we are going through. I come from a long line of thinkers who believe that economic science is important and that we will ultimately be able to deal with the incredible highs and lows of money itself. The issue is always application.

The US dollar has served as a de facto international currency for many years, and arguments are being made in support of the euro taking its place. However, true reform would require that an international currency have the backing and stability of gold reserves. The fiat system has never worked, and today's fiat money will not work permanently, either.

CRYPTO EVANGELISM

On December, 13, 2022, Samuel Bankman-Fried (SBF), the founder of the cryptocurrency exchange FTX, was arrested in the Bahamas for wire fraud, money laundering, and a host of other charges that one journalist calculated could total a sentence, if convicted on all counts, of 612,000 years in prison. The sentencing potential is as unbelievable as the cryptocurrency bubble itself.

When we began writing *Demise of the Dollar* in 2005. . . even when we updated and revised the book in 2008. . . cryptocurrencies were a gleam in someone's eye. We've had many editors write countless words praising the idea that Bitcoin, as the brand-label and proxy for crypto currencies, could stand against the fiat currency system we've been writing about.

The introduction of all new technologies, in this case block chain, which is the technology behind Bitcoin and other cryptos, is subject to fraud, abuse, and fantasy. It's too early in this book to find out what's going to come out of the SBF trial. . . or his connection to the greatest quarterback in NFL history, Tom Brady, or his then soon to be ex-wife, supermodel, Giselle Bundchen.

As of this writing, SBF is sitting in a dank prison cell in the Bahamas. His lawyers are allegedly making the argument that he needs to be extradited to the United States because the prison conditions, even Riker's Island, are safer and "they don't trust the Bahamian government."[17]

The story of FTX and its sister company, Alameda Research, run by Sam Bankman-Fried's girlfriend Carolina Allison, is just beginning to unfold. The Scottish economic historian Niall Ferguson likened it to the massive fraud uncovered during the Mississippi Scheme in the early 1700s, with Bankman-Fried playing the role of John Law.[18] (We addressed John Law in our book *Financial Reckoning Day*, which we'll be updating early in 2023.)

The whole crypto episode, including its most famous component Bitcoin, is only a decade and a half old, which makes it both new and interesting. Many of its ardent evangelists believe it is the policy-free alternative to paper money and government control. And it begs the following question.[19]

WHAT IS MONEY, ANYWAY?

It is a store of value.

Perhaps a paper money system pegged specifically to commodity reserves would give the currency the stability it needs and rein in government spending. But we don't really know. Since 1971, we rely on "the full faith and credit" of the US government, as we have explained. We rely on press conferences and the "minutes" from the meetings held by the Federal Reserve governors to determine what the dollar is "worth."

We need stable money to give entrepreneurs, innovators, and business leaders the guidance for how and when to invest. A fiat currency system is subject to central banks. So, by extension, business is dependent on the policy determined at the Fed. For someone like me trying to run a publishing company, it's annoying. We spend a lot of time trying to interpret signals from the Fed. As do homeowners and parents trying to pay for ever rising tuition payments.

THE TWILIGHT OF THE GREAT DOLLAR STANDARD ERA

American consumers face the specter of losing value in their retirement savings, finding out they cannot live on a fixed income, and suffering from chronic hyperinflation. These changes are unavoidable.

Today, the problem is compounded because the US dollar's value is falling. It all involves productivity changes in the United States. We have not competed with the manufacturing economies in other countries, and that is why our credit (i.e., our dollar) is suffering.

Any number of things could create a sudden, wrenching drop in the dollar's value. Consider the following three possibilities:

1. *Foreign countries drop their US dollar reserves.* We depend on foreign investment in our currency to bolster its value or, at least, to slow down its fall. When that thinly held balance changes, our dollar loses its spending power. In February 2005, South Korea announced that it will stop holding US dollars and bonds in its reserves—but that was only the beginning. In an odd twist of financial fate, on the same day that the Canadian loonie[20] achieved parity with the US dollar, Saudi Arabia refused to adjust rates in lockstep with the Federal Reserve. Keeping its interest rate unchanged may signal Saudi Arabia's desire to break its dollar peg. Iran, Iraq, and Kuwait have already dumped the dollar; will the Saudis be next? At a November 2007 meeting of the Organization of Petroleum Exporting Countries's 13-member cartel, Iranian President Mahmoud Ahmadinejad, whose country already receives payment for 85% of its oil exports in nondollar currencies, urged other countries to follow suit and "designate a single hard currency aside from the US dollar . . . to form the basis of our oil trade." "The empire of the dollar has to end," chimed in Venezuela's Hugo Chavez; his state oil company changed its dollar investments to euros at his order—er, request.

   Rumors are circulating that the Bank of Korea, after selling off $100 million worth of US bonds in August 2007, is getting ready to sell $1 billion more, and if Washington forces trade sanctions, China, which threatened recently to cash in $900 billion of US bonds, will probably follow suit. In Russia, Vladimir Putin's dream of a stock market to trade the country's natural resources in rubles is not so far-fetched; in 2005, Russia, the world's second-largest exporter of oil, followed South Korea's lead and ended the dollar peg. And once again,

Sudan is hinting that it will impose trade or financial sanctions against companies that do business with the United States—only this time, the words just might have teeth.

As other countries follow suit, the dollar—and your spending power—drops. What does this mean? You will need more dollars to buy things than it takes today.

2. *Oil prices increase catastrophically.* We—and our real inflation rate—are at the mercy of Middle East oil. In 2005, we couldn't imagine what would happen if the price of oil were to double—or triple, but that's exactly what has happened in 2007 as oil kept flirting with $100-a-barrel prices. Our vulnerability is not imaginary. For example, if terrorists were to contaminate large reserves with nuclear radiation, the supply of oil would drop, and prices would rise. We are all aware of our vulnerability and dependence on oil, but we don't like to think about it. Rising oil prices affect not only what you pay at the pump, but many other prices as well: nonautomotive modes of travel, the cost of utilities, and local tax rates, for example. It all adds up to unquestioned "pain at the pump" for American consumers. By September 2007, gasoline averaged $2.78 a gallon—double 2002's price. "Pain at the pump" leads to "pain in the pocketbook," as consumers know. You're not seeing double in the checkout line at the grocery store—costs really *are* double. There was a 5.6% increase in 2007, compared with 2.1% for all of 2006.

3. *The double whammy of trade and budget deficits.* We're living beyond our means. It's as simple as that, and something is going to give. The federal budget deficit—annual government spending that is higher than tax revenues—adds to the national debt at a dizzying rate, making our future interest burden higher and higher every day. Our trade deficit—bringing more things in from foreign countries than we sell to the same countries—has turned us into a nation of spendaholics. We've given up making things to sell elsewhere, closed the store, and gone shopping. But we're not spending money we have; we're *borrowing* money to spend it. In 2006, the trade and budget deficits doubled the deficits of 2001. Any head of

a family knows that this cannot go on forever without the whole thing falling apart—and yet, that is precisely what we are doing on a national scale.

Even as the US economy overheats, political leaders get out their fiddles. They point to economic indicators to prove that the economy is strong and getting stronger. The message would be valuable . . . if only it were true.

Politicians like to measure the economy with esoteric indicators. For example, we are told that consumer confidence is up. Well, confidence is all well and good, but what if it isn't accurate? Yankee optimism has achieved a lot in the past 200 years, but it alone is not going to prevent the current dollar crisis from getting worse and worse.

Does this mean that the United States is finished? No, but it does mean that our long history of economic power and wealth is being eroded from within. For example, look at how the reality has affected you in recent years. For most people, the real state of our economy is measured in one way: *jobs*. Sure, the number of jobs rises every month, but the complete truth is not as reassuring. We are losing *high-paying* jobs in manufacturing and replacing them with *low-paying* jobs in health care, retail, and other menial job markets. Our mantra of "Yankee ingenuity can accomplish anything" is gradually being replaced with a new mantra: "Would you like fries with that?"

As manufacturing jobs continue to move to China and India, and elsewhere around the globe, you would think we'd tighten our belts. But instead, we increase our debt to spend more.

Few people, even those who consider themselves to be savvy about finance, really understand things like the trade deficit, national debt, gross domestic product, inflation, economic indicators, and the like.

The truth (one few investors want to hear) is that your local member of Congress is often just as illiterate about economics as most of us are, but the difference is that he or she has the power and position to make decisions that affect you. And he or she may be making the *wrong* decisions. You, like many other Americans, may have put aside income every month in a variety of retirement plans, long-term investments, and savings, in the belief that this is going to provide security in your old age. What are they going to be worth when you retire? Given the current state of things, you could find out that your retirement accounts are going to be worth next to nothing.

This is not the time to rush out and buy more stocks, for example, or to load up on new bargains in the property market. Quite the opposite. The subprime mess isn't over. Foreclosures keep growing. In December of 2007, we stopped believing the forecasts from the National Association of REALTORS® (NAR), which declared a market rebound in early 2008. When the NAR revised their 2007 sales forecast for existing homes the ninth consecutive month and, by our count, the tenth time that year, we officially called B.S. Making a 2007 forecast in the middle of December is lame enough. But when it's your tenth revision in 12 months, it's not even fair to call it a forecast.

So where should you invest? Read on. We provide you with the specifics about what's really going on with the dollar and our economy, how foreign countries ultimately control our economic fate, and how our leaders are deceiving us by telling us that we're in good shape. Finally, we offer strategies you can employ today to not only protect your financial freedom but to prosper in a dollar demise.

FROM KNOW-HOW TO NOWHERE

Back to Triffin's paradox. The first thing to realize about a deficit in foreign trade is that, by definition, it reflects an excess of domestic spending over domestic output. But such spending excess is actually caused by overly liberal credit at home, and not really by cheaper goods produced elsewhere.

Just as shaky is the second argument, ascribing the trade gap to higher US economic growth. Asian countries, in particular China, have much higher rates of economic growth than the United States. Yet they all run a chronic trade surplus, which is caused by high savings rates. This is the crucial variable concerning trade surplus or trade deficit.

The diversion of US domestic spending to foreign producers is, in effect, a loss of revenue for businesses and consumers in the United States. Is this important? Yes. The loss in 2021 was a heart-stopping $845 billion.[21] This is America's income and profit killer, and it can't be fixed with *more* credit and *more* consumption. This serious drag of the growing trade gap on US domestic incomes and profits would have bred slower economic growth, if not recession, long ago. This has so far been delayed by the Fed's extreme monetary looseness, creating artificial domestic demand growth through credit expansion.

The need for ever-greater credit and debt creation just to offset the income losses caused by the trade gap is one of our big problems. An equally big problem is a distortion of the numbers. We are officially in great shape, but the numbers don't support this belief. Personal consumption in the past few years has increased real GDP at the expense of savings, while business investment has grown only moderately.

This can only end badly. Normally, tight money forces consumers and businesses to unwind their excesses during recessions. But in the latest round, the Fed's loose monetary stance has *stepped up* consumers' spending excesses. Our weight trainer is feeding us Big Macs. If we were to measure economic health by credit expansion, the United States has the worst inflation in history. And still our experts are puzzled by a soaring import surplus.

The problem here is that American policy makers and economists fail to understand the significance of the damage that is being caused by monetary excess and the growing trade gap. The trade gap is hailed as a sign of superior economic growth, while the hyperinflation in stock and house prices is hailed as wealth creation.

Until the late 1960s, total international reserves of central banks hovered below $100 billion. At the end of 2003, they exceeded $3 trillion, of which two-thirds was held in dollars. And starting in 2001, the rapid buildup exploded. Foreign reserves now are estimated at $5.6 trillion—but reserves don't include sovereign wealth funds (SWFs), government-owned or -controlled funds, which add another $1.5 trillion to $2.7 trillion. A steep jump in these reserves, an increase of $907 billion, occurred in the years 2000–2002, when Asian central banks, with China and Japan as the main buyers, bought virtually the whole amount. And despite global ups and downs, these two countries are still buying.

And who said economists don't have a sense of humor? In early 2006, before leaving the White House Council of Economic Advisers and joining the Fed as its new chairman, Ben Bernanke suggested that the growing US trade deficit—a bubble the size of 6% of our

GDP—was not really a deficit but a "savings glut," caused by excessive saving in Asia and Europe. So we can conveniently blame our growing US trade deficit on the rest of the world, which saves too much. It's *their* fault for selling us stuff and then putting all the cash they earn back in the US of A.

It was widely assumed that rising stock and house prices would keep American consumers both willing and able to spend, spend, spend their way to wealth—indefinitely. But that assumption radically changed in 2007, when the housing bubble finally burst.

Also alarming is the transfer of US net worth to interests overseas, which endangers US economic and political health. Case in point: Warren Buffett, who kept his vast fortune invested at home for more than 70 years, decided in 2002 to invest in foreign currencies for the first time. Buffett and the management of Berkshire Hathaway believe the dollar is going to continue its decline. We should not need confirmation such as this to recognize the inevitable, but it bolsters the argument that the dollar is, in fact, in serious trouble, and that this trouble is likely to continue. In addition to debt problems at home, Buffett made his decision based at least partially on the ever-growing trade deficit. In his most recent letter to Berkshire Hathaway shareholders, Buffett warned:

> As our US trade problems worsen, the probability that the dollar will weaken over time continues to be high. I fervently believe in real trade—the more the better for both us and the world. We had about $1.44 trillion of this honest-to-God trade in 2006. But the US also had $.76 trillion of *pseudo*-trade last year—imports for which we exchanged no goods or services

> Making these purchases that weren't reciprocated by sales, the US necessarily transferred ownership of its assets or IOUs to the rest of the world. Like a very wealthy but self-indulgent family, we peeled off a bit of what we owned in order to consume more than we produced.[22]

Buffett has been especially concerned about the transfer of wealth to outside interests. He notes:

> These transfers will have consequences, however. Already the prediction I made last year about one fall-out from our spending binge

has come true: The "investment income" account of our country—positive in every previous year since 1915—turned negative in 2006. Foreigners now earn more on their US investments than we do on our investments abroad. In effect, we've used up our bank account and turned to our credit card. And, like everyone who gets in hock, the US will now experience "reverse compounding" as we pay ever-increasing amounts of interest on interest.[23]

CHAPTER 8

ALAS, THE DEMISE OF THE DOLLAR

When written in Chinese, the word crisis *is composed of two characters. One represents danger and the other represents opportunity.*

—*John F. Kennedy*

The global economy is continuing to change, as it will. The US dollar remains on the front lines of change as its reserve currency, for now. When we take a look at history, we see how past events have affected everything. The Black Death created a devastating labor shortage throughout Europe for decades. Christopher Columbus's voyages turned trade upside down for hundreds of years. The industrial revolution moved economic power in ways that continue to affect economic balances to this day. And now we face another great shift, away from US dominance of world markets and toward new leaders—China and India.

The economic reality—a type of geography—is changing. As a consequence, real estate speculation in New York, Chicago, and Los Angeles may be replaced with more global interest in the new real estate markets—in Beijing, Shanghai, and Bombay. Who knows? We can only anticipate how changes will occur based on what we observe today. Does this mean the age of America is ending? No, it simply means that economic muscle will be flexed by someone else in the future. This is a trend. And like all trends, they are more easily viewed in historical perspective but harder to judge from their midst.

When we look at trends in dollar values, we can observe that incomes have not declined. That's great. But we also see that prices have risen faster than incomes. So with decreased buying power (caused by this disparity) we *have* seen a decline in income in terms of what really counts. It takes more dollars to buy the same thing (in other words, prices are higher), but incomes have not risen to meet that price inflation. That's what happens when the value of the dollar declines.

Economic history is a history of bubbles—and of bursts. The great disservice being done to Americans by the financial media is that they are not being offered the opportunity to learn from what is going on. They are losing buying power, but apart from a few painful spikes at the gas pumps and in grocery lines, it's invisible.

In the Great Dollar Standard Era, the problem is global. While there is, of course, more to it than just the value of the US dollar, here is how it works. Fake money creates fake demand.

The global economy is interconnected. Even as early as the 1930s, we saw the impact of how an economic challenge in the United States could create a worldwide depression. The Great Depression resulted from multiple causes, but most notable among them were two things: a huge transfer of funds from World War I reparations and far too much credit that went beyond the borrowers' ability to repay. All of that credit—essentially, funny money—also created a fake demand. We see the effects of this policy in housing as severely as anywhere.

The whole mess is traced back to the origin—a Fed policy encouraging debt spending as a means to artificially create the appearance of productivity.

It has always been an effective policy to raise rates to slow down inflation, just as lead rods are moved into the radioactive core of a reactor to cool down the chain reaction. Higher rates put a damper on spending. This has been recognized widely, so the Fed policy—based on the idea that lower rates are "good for the economy"—is without merit. In fact, it is damaging. The housing market and the mortgage bubble bursting in 2008—and the following subprime mortgage mess and credit crisis—were the first victims of this policy and the most visible.

Then the Fed persisted and insisted on keeping rates below market value for another decade. The trouble with the Fed keeping rates low as long as it did after the crisis had been averted was that it wasn't prepared for the next crisis when it would invariably hit. In our lucky case, it was a global virus that, through a concerted worldwide policy effort, shuttered the entire global economy.

THE WEAKENING DOLLAR AND ITS EFFECT ON THE ECONOMY

In the first edition, we said that the day was surely coming when foreign investors will reach a limit in their willingness to buy US debt, thus financing our deficit. The finance minister of India hinted as much in late 2004. South Korea, too, made overtures for reducing the amount of US dollars it holds in reserve. Well, that day arrived. In August 2007, the central banks of Japan, China, and Taiwan sold US Treasuries at the fastest rate in as many as seven years. Taiwan cut nearly 9% of its Treasury holdings, its biggest sell-off since 2000. China shed more than 2%, its biggest move since 2002. And Japan dumped 4% of its US Treasuries, its largest reduction since 2002.

A few months later, in November 2007, the US Treasury's TIC data revealed that Japan, China, Caribbean banking centers, Luxembourg, Hong Kong, South Korea, Germany, Singapore, Mexico, Switzerland, Turkey, Canada, the Netherlands, Sweden, France, Russia, Ireland, and Israel were all net sellers of US Treasuries in September. For three months in a row, Japan and China—the world's largest holders of US government debt—were sellers of such Treasuries. They now hold less than $1 trillion in dollar reserves. The central banks of these countries will conclude that it's smart to move their funds into other currencies—or to demand higher returns on their money.

We have all heard of *denial*—that self-protective tendency to contradict the obvious truth. Well, our federal policy makers are suffering from denial. Drunk on the power of the dollar and heedless of the damage it does to print more and more currency, our leaders have convinced themselves of something: that if the dollar's value falls, that will eliminate the trade deficit, reduce inflation, and improve our GDP. Just as onetime fiscal conservative Richard Nixon decided to try wage and price controls to solve the economic problems of 1971 and then took the US economy off the gold standard, this new but illogical plan will also fail.

The United States has seen little to low growth in manufacturing (defined in terms of number of jobs, output, or profits) in more than 20 years. Changing this situation is the only solution to the trade deficit. In other words, we have to compete. We cannot trick the economy into coming into line by reducing the value of the dollar. It was possible on the gold standard to control economic trends to a degree. But we cannot simply look for easy solutions. Destroying our own currency's buying power is not the answer.

In fact, before we actually lost our trading dominance, the dollar wasn't worth too much compared to other currencies. Nixon's economic decisions were based on the realization that some prices were unrealistically low, coupled with the fear that not correcting that problem could cost him re-election. Unfortunately, he did not stop with wage and price controls and a tariff surcharge. He proceeded as though the problem had been created by the dollar, and that simply was not the case.

Between 1984 and 1994, total consumer credit in the United States grew from $527 billion to $1.021 trillion (almost doubling in the decade). From 1994 through 2007, the debt rose to $2.480 trillion, doubling again at an accelerated rate. Check the graph in Figure 8.1.

In the years from 1984 to 1994, the average annual growth in consumer debt was $49.4 billion per year. In the next decade, though, the average rate was $108.3 billion and moved upward year after year at that faster rate. In the third quarter of 2007, consumer debt pushed close to $2.5 trillion—a 25% increase in less than three years. But that's only the tip of the proverbial iceberg: The real danger lies in the credit crisis beneath the surface.

It's eerie—in December 2004, we ran the playfully facetious headline, "The Total Destruction of the US Housing Market." Little did we know how right we were. The crux of our argument at the time was that Fannie Mae, the nation's biggest—and government-backed—enabler of the subprime mortgage market, was in trouble. We retell it here as a cautionary tale.

Internally, Fannie Mae had published a report revealing the firm's exposure to the derivatives market. The author of the report was

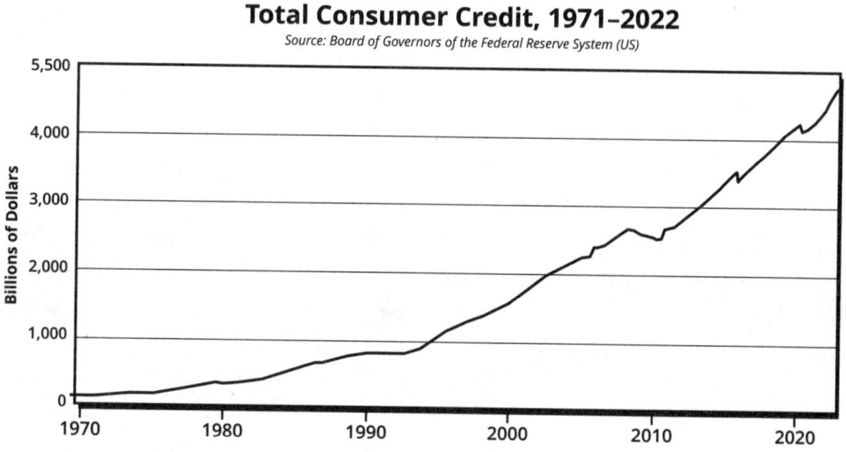

Total Consumer Credit, 1971–2022

Source: Board of Governors of the Federal Reserve System (US)

FIGURE 8.1 Consumer Credit Outstanding, 1971–2022

Source: Board of Governors of the Federal Reserve System (US)

reprimanded and fired, and the report mysteriously disappeared from the internet. Fannie had been engaged in Enron-style accounting. Heck, it even used Arthur Andersen as its accountant—the same firm used by Enron. Congressional hearings followed, but all was soon completely forgotten—until the news surfaced about the fallout with Freddie.

Until the secondary market for mortgage-backed securities started drying up over the summer of 2007, Freddie Mac and Fannie Mae—which own or guarantee about 40% of the $11.5 trillion residential mortgage market in this country—were the reliable sources of credit that kept the pulse beating. Now Freddie is telling us that if conditions continue to deteriorate, it may have to purchase fewer mortgages, which would take even more homebuyers out of the market.

As if on cue, the worst home sales report of all time was issued the same day. Existing home sales fell 20% in October 2007 from the previous October, to an annual rate of 4.9 million, the lowest ever recorded by the National Association of REALTORS® (NAR). October also marked the 15th out of the past 17 months in which this price measure posted a year-over-year decline. And wouldn't you know—a record level of homes are now sitting in inventory, a whopping 11-month supply.

Given the massive acceleration in rate of credit expansion, it does not seem likely that a falling dollar is going to fix the problem of the trade deficit. This credit money, which is not backed by anything, can best be described as "magical, out-of-thin-air fairy dust money."[1] One saving grace in today's economy is that our trading partners and competitors are in bed with us, economically. In the 1980s, overseas dollar-based assets held by foreign interests were practically at zero. Today, those holdings have ballooned to about $16.295 trillion. So our fortunes—including the value of the dollar—have ramifications for heavily invested foreign central banks and private interests.

THE THREAT OF INFLATION—OH, WAIT, IT'S HERE

The United States has enjoyed such low inflation for many years (compared to the late 1970s, at least) that many Americans came to believe that inflation was a thing of the past. Ironically, some people even credited the Fed and its monetary policies with controlling or ending inflation.

This is 180 degrees from the truth. We have inflation, but the credit-based economy and liberal monetary policies of the Fed kept inflation pent up. Experience and history both tell us that these aberrations

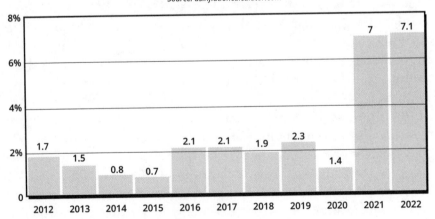

Inflation in the United States, 2013–2022

Source: usinflationcalculator.com

FIGURE 8.2 Inflation in the United States, 2013–2022

Source: usinflationcalculator.com

eventually become realized, usually with a vengeance. And that's exactly what we saw during and following the pandemic (*See* Figure 8.2).

We have to remember that inflation and the falling dollar are in fact the same thing, but expressed in different ways. So the Fed's policies are designed to keep interest rates and inflation down while encouraging consumer debt to rise—all on the premise that this will stimulate investment and growth. At the same time that the Fed wants to continue to see a falling dollar, it claims it is fighting to ward off inflation. The two goals are at odds with one another.

The financial media got in the habit of listening to Bernanke during his tenure. Yellen continued the now Nobel-prize-winning economist's logic. He had a way of framing bad news that is reminiscent of many corporate annual reports. Their philosophy that economic news must always be expressed in positive tones tends to obscure what is really going on. And did so for more than a decade. It wasn't until Jerome Powell was faced with near double digit inflation that the Fed tone changed. We haven't found any evidence where the Fed governors have taken accountability for causing the inflation they're now hawkish about battling.

In December 2006, Bernanke traveled to Beijing to talk to the Chinese about their economy. He duly noted China's "impressive rate" of growth, of 9% a year from 1990 to 2005.[2] But that's nothing compared to the growth in trade that occurred after China joined the World Trade Organization in 2001, when the dollar value of exports started growing at an average annual rate of about 30%. Add in capital inflows—particularly foreign direct investment (FDI), which leaped from $2 billion in 1986 to $72 billion by 2005—and you're looking at a pretty robust picture.

But there's a flaw, Bernanke told his audience: The Chinese are investing and saving too much. Approximately 33% of their GDP goes into fixed business investment, and the national savings rate is way into the ozone, at 52%—compared to our now below–zero rate. That kind of behavior is contributing to "global imbalances," the Fed head told the Chinese gravely. The solution: Increase monetary and social policies "aimed at increasing household consumption." In other words: Get debt.

It's amazing just how much Bernanke, then Yellen after him, sounded like the old bespectacled boss. In fact, the Greenspan era, which lasted from 1987 to 2006, set the stage for everything we saw and heard for the ensuing 12 years. To understand just how important Alan Greenspan's influence was, it's helpful to reread him.

In January 2004, Greenspan explained that our trade gap with China (while still a deficit) had narrowed. He explained that "following a shortfall of $41.6 billion a month earlier . . . the trade deficit with China narrowed to $10.8 billion from $13.6 billion."[3]

Great news, Mr. G. The Fed chairman's policy of "salvation by devaluation" was reflected momentarily in reduced trade gap numbers. But are these truly related? While reducing the dollar's value is unavoidably inflationary (by definition, a lower dollar *is* inflation), it boggles the mind to accept Greenspan's argument. In essence, he claimed that inflation creates lower trade deficits. He has never admitted that a devalued dollar and inflation are the same animal, but anyone who has survived an Economics 101 class knows that it is. We have cleaned up inflation by calling it something else. We have put lipstick on the pig and called it by another name.

In fact, Greenspan shrugged off concerns about the falling dollar. He said that he expected current global currency imbalances would be easily diffused with little or no disruption.[4] He referred to flexibility in international policy as the key to this easy fix. On January 13, 2004, Greenspan spoke in Berlin: "The greater the degree of international flexibility, the less the risk of a crisis."

He also set up the European economies as the fall guy for the effects of the falling dollar, thus a rising euro, saying that any protectionist initiatives among European nations would erode the flexibility. In the same talk, Greenspan—perhaps in a fit of denial?—commented that US current account deficits were not a problem. Here again, he obscured the relationship between a falling dollar and inflation, stating that it was true the US dollar had fallen against other nations' currencies, but at the same time inflation "appears quiescent."

Greenspan's cryptic warning concerning where this all goes contradicts his claim to a quiescent inflation. He went on to explain that if the current deficit were allowed to continue, "at some point in the future further adjustments will be set in motion that will eventually slow and presumably reverse" demand from foreign investors for US debt, a prediction that looks very possible lately.

At that time, the US trade deficit sat at about 5% of GDP. Greenspan shrugged this off as well, even in the face of rising deficits over time. He claimed that financing the US debt with US dollars would, in essence, expand the US ability to carry debt. Or, putting it another way—if we understood Greenspan correctly—our dollar is so popular that it serves to increase our international line of credit. This sounds like the policy of deficit spending—no big deal, apparently—should only continue and expand.

In fact, Greenspan's opening statement during his January 2004 speech is amazing in itself:

> Globalization has altered the economic frameworks of both developed and developing nations in ways that are difficult to fully comprehend. Nonetheless, the largely unregulated global markets do clear and, with rare exceptions, appear to move effortlessly from one state of equilibrium to another. It is as though an international version of Adam Smith's "invisible hand" is at work.[5]

The "invisible hand" was Adam Smith's metaphor referring to an economic principle of "enlightened self-interest." The theory supports a contention that in a capitalist system, the individual works for his own good, but also tends to work for the good of the nation or community as well:

> Every individual necessarily labors to render the annual revenue of the society as great as he can. He generally neither intends to promote the public interest, nor knows how much he is promoting it. He intends only his own gain, and he is in this, as in many other cases, led by an invisible hand to promote an end which was no part of his intention. Nor is it always the worse for society than if it was no part of his intention. By pursuing his own interest he frequently promotes that of the society more effectually than when he really intends to promote it. I have never known much good done by those who affected to trade for the public good.[6]

Greenspan latched onto this argument, made originally by Smith to argue against regulation and protectionism in markets. But the unintended consequences of the principle are disturbing if, as

Mr. Greenspan claims, the international monetary situation depends on governments doing less rather than more. The Fed chairman had more praise for Adam Smith a year later in the Adam Smith Memorial Lecture in Fife, Scotland. He described Smith as "a towering contributor to the development of the modern world." He expressed the belief in Smith's principles of an unregulated market, in an apparent reference to modern trends in international trade and notably China. Greenspan said, "A large majority of developing nations quietly shifted to more market-oriented economies."[7]

Let's not forget, it was the United States that went off the gold standard—arguably to remove the restrictive nature of pegging money to gold, but in practice to enable a planned intervention in international trade by expanding the dollar. That in itself was and still is a form of protectionism, the very thing Greenspan argued against. If US policy was truly faithful to the idea of unregulated international monetary policy, it would have left the gold standard in place, recognizing it as a means for curtailing runaway inflation, jarring monetary disparities, and—as we now have—huge deficits. In spite of the Fed theme to the contrary, printing money and creating a debt-based economy is contrary to Smith's hypothesis.

Greenspan had a theory about the huge US current account deficits. But he dismissed it in one respect by pointing out that deficits and surpluses always balance out:

> Although for the world as a whole the sum of surpluses must always match the sum of deficits, the combined size of both, relative to global gross domestic product, has grown markedly since the end of World War II. This trend is inherently sustainable unless some countries build up deficits that are no longer capable of being financed.[8]

Hmm. As in the case of the United States perhaps? What Greenspan is saying here is that growing deficits are no problem unless they get so large that the lender nations—those with net surplus dollars—are no longer willing to carry the debt. This is clearly the simplest method by which to judge a nation's economic health. If the size of the current account deficit has gotten too large, it is easy to see that the country is living beyond its means—and the trend cannot continue without dire consequences. However, it appeared that Greenspan was not aware of this. He continued:

> There is no simple measure by which to judge the sustainability of either a string of current account deficits or their consequences, a significant buildup in external claims that need to be serviced. In the end, the restraint on the size of tolerable US imbalances in the global arena will likely be the reluctance of foreign country residents to accumulate additional debt and equity claims against US residents.[9]

In fact, as Greenspan pointed out in the same speech, the trend is certainly heading to that obvious but dire conclusion. He noted that by the end of 2003, net external claims had grown to about 25% of US GDP, with average annual growth continuing at 5% per year. But, he contends, "the sustainability of the current account deficit is difficult to estimate." Why, we wonder, is it so difficult? Greenspan double-speaks by explaining that US capacity for increased debt is "a function of globalization since the apparent increase in our debt-raising capacity appears to be related to the reduced cost and increasing reach of international financial intermediation."[10]

Well, that statement makes no sense, but here's what really matters. Any American who holds a mortgage knows where it goes if he or she keeps borrowing on the equity. Your bank wants you to have 20% equity in your home, for example, but you sign up for a series of additional mortgages, a line of credit, and refinancing of your paper equity. At some point your debt is 125% of equity, and then what? Will your lender institute some form of "financial intermediation" by saying, for example, "no more debt"? If a lender draws the line at that point, then your capacity to borrow will be stopped. This is where the US debt trend is going, and Greenspan admitted as much in the statement (even though no one can be sure about what he really meant).

Greenspan seemed to earnestly believe in his theme, that "market forces" would work in a flexible world economy to make everything all right. Does this mean the deficits will simply disappear? No, but it does imply that the *level* of deficits is acceptable given those very market forces—and that these levels will become even more acceptable in the future. Somehow. It's a matter of *flexibility* in his view that will lead to this improvement in the state of US debt. He said:

> Can market forces incrementally defuse a worrisome buildup in a nation's current account deficit and net external debt before a crisis abruptly does so? The answer seems to lie with the degree of flexibility in both domestic and international markets. By flexibility I mean the ability of an economy to absorb shocks, stabilize, and recover. In domestic economies that approach full flexibility, imbalances are likely to be adjusted well before they become potentially destabilizing. In a similar flexible world economy, as debt projections rise, product and equity prices, interest rates, and exchange rates could change, presumably to reestablish global balance.[11]

And if only the rest of the world would go along with US policy in other regards, we could all have peace and prosperity. But that isn't going to happen. It's more likely that the invisible hand is going to slap us across the face with a monetary rude awakening.

Greenspan refers to the "paradigm of flexibility" in a stated desire to see exchange rates stabilize. But doesn't that sound like what Nixon was trying to accomplish in 1971 by going off the gold standard? To any extent, what he was trying to accomplish didn't work. It only led to the current mess in terms of the trade deficit and the falling dollar.

Greenspan's speech was revealing, not only in demonstrating his economic philosophy but also in showing his view of how economic forces work. His dismissal of growing debt as a significant force ignored the important differences between *spending* borrowed funds and *investing* borrowed funds. Apparently he didn't believe the distinction to be an important one, and neither does his successor. The problem is—and it's a big problem as 2007 draws to a close—the fiscal environment has changed. Inflation is much more of a threat, but Bernanke doesn't have the luxury of following in Greenspan's footsteps. In fact, Greenspan said so to *USA Today* in an interview published on September 14, 2007, to promote his autobiography. "We had the luxury of not worrying too much on the downside." But now, "That luxury is gone. So Ben [Bernanke] is going to have a tougher time, more difficult decisions, than I had."

INFLATION BY ANY OTHER NAME

If you define *inflation* as an expansion of the money supply (which, of course, devalues the dollar through dilution, at the very least), you need to also look beyond this definition. We are facing a new kind of inflation: *price inflation.*

Higher prices are a reflection of decreased purchasing power of our dollars. It is academic to argue which method of explanation is more accurate. Under widespread price inflation, it takes more money to buy the same stuff.

We should not ignore the extreme hyperinflation of Germany in the 1920s as an example of how bad things can become when inflation gets out of control. In January 1919, an ounce of gold cost 170 German marks. Less than five years later, the same ounce cost 87 *billion* marks. The hyperinflation affected everything, even postage stamps. We have seen a similar type of inflationary effect in many other countries. Toward the end of the USSR empire, a worker was interviewed in Moscow during a time when some employers were paying workers in clay bricks rather than currency. When asked about the situation, a worker told a reporter, "We pretend to work, and they pretend to pay us."

A devalued currency—or, in the extreme, a worthless currency—is going to affect where and how we invest. It will affect far more than prices, perhaps requiring everyone—even the securely delusional American consumer—to rethink the whole attitude toward money, spending, and debt.

As we've noted, one important sign of the weakening dollar and currency inflation is seen in the price of gold. Tracking gold prices is a reliable way to gauge what is going on with currency values, because the tendency is for gold's value to rise as the dollar value falls.

A historical example from the last period of dollar weakening will help us here. Following the great Tech Wreck, the crash in tech stocks that began March 10, 2000, when the Nasdaq stock market index peaked at 5,132.52, gold began to rise off its 1999 low of $253. By 2003 the price rose above the magic $400 per ounce level for the first time in eight years. By 2004, the gold price had grown 25% in one year and was up 60% from its low point in 1999. Almost as good as gold is the opinion of those in the know, such as Warren Buffett. In 2003, for the first time in his life, Buffett began buying foreign currencies—to the tune of $12 billion by year-end. He cited continuing weakness in the US dollar as the reason.[12]

By the beginning of 2005, Buffett was still betting against the dollar. His foreign currency holdings increased to $20 billion. At the time he began buying up overseas currency, the euro was worth 86 cents to the US dollar. By January 2005, the euro traded at $1.33, an improvement of more than 50%, and it continued its upward climb. So is Buffett smart to change his strategy? In the first three quarters of 2004, his company, Berkshire Hathaway, netted $207 million on currency speculation—not bad. Looking back at the fall of the dollar against the euro—33% between 2002 and 2005—it would seem that Buffett's timing was great. Since 2002, he has scooped up $2.2 billion for his shareholders. In his famous plain-speaking way, he explained his concerns about the value of the US dollar: "If we have the same policies, the dollar will go down."[13]

In fact, Buffett told us in person recently, "If the current account deficit continues, the dollar will be worth less 5 to 10 years from now."

"Insanity consists of doing the same thing over and over again and expecting a different result," quoted the sage. "In the United States, the cause, in my view, of the declining dollar in very major part, is the current account deficit, and the trade deficit being the biggest part in that." He went on to say, "I don't know what it will look like in any short term, but I would say that force-feeding a couple billion a day to the rest of the world is inconsistent with a stable dollar."

In a Q&A session with the *Financial Post,* Buffett admitted he had made "several hundred million" bucks buying Canadian loonies over the past year, a position that he also admitted he regretted leaving.

Today, Buffett says he currently owns only two currencies: the embattled greenback and Brazilian real. The dollar, suffice to say, hasn't been treating him well. Buffett didn't disclose when he bought reals, so we can only guess how he's done on that one.

Buffett's change to foreign currencies is significant. When the Oracle of Omaha does something he has never done before, it's worth noting.

Why, though, has he decided on this big shift now? Buffett is concerned with the huge (and growing) balance of payments deficit. Foreign investors hold $9 trillion in US debt, consisting of bonds and other debts. He sees the day in the not so distant future when this buying spree will end. Because the US economy depends on continued overseas investment (as a means of financing our debt economy), any slowdown in the volume will result in further weakening of the dollar. In other words, it can't go on forever.

Buffett isn't the only guru who saw the problem in clear terms. George Soros, Sir John Templeton, Jim Rogers, and Bill Gates all agreed. In other words, many investment luminaries known for their good timing and vision are in agreement that the dollar is in big trouble. In a nutshell, a weakened dollar is a relative matter, so it means that other currencies will perform better and will strengthen. Even Alan Greenspan knows that all things equal out, whether trade imbalances, deficits and surpluses, or currency values.

THE FED'S PREDICTABLE COURSE, REVISED

Fed policy is, in fact, an intrinsic part of the path toward a falling dollar—not only by inevitable consequences, but as part of a stated federal policy. The Fed wants the dollar to fall, in theory and in practice. It's easier to pay off debt if there are more dollars in the system, even if that means the dollar buys less for you. Jerome Powell, as the chairman of the Fed, has been making bold statements about raising rates until inflation is under control. But with the debt situation the government has gotten itself into, it actually makes sense to inflate the currency. In past economic practice, allowing interest rates to rise was the effective means for curbing excess spending. Today, spending isn't viewed as a problem. A review of Fed history explains how we've gotten to this point.

As we've noted, the Federal Reserve was first suggested in 1907 by Paul Warburg, publisher of the *New York Times Annual Financial Review*. Warburg suggested the formation of a central banking system to help deter panics. One of Warburg's partners, Jacob Schiff, warned the same year that lacking such a central bank, the country would "undergo the most severe and far reaching money panic in its history."[14]

They were both right in their prediction. The infamous Panic of 1907 hit in October. The idea that panics were caused, at least in part, by lack of strong central banking controls continues to find considerable support. Even Milton Friedman (with Anna J. Schwartz) is on record in believing that the Great Depression was as severe as it was primarily because the Federal Reserve mismanaged the nation's money supply.[15]

To help us sum up, we need to review the responsibilities of the Fed to understand where we are today. The Fed was authorized to undertake three primary roles: supervise and regulate banks, implement monetary policy by buying and selling US Treasury bonds, and maintain a strong payments system. Operating as a central bank (organized with its 12 regional reserve banks, a Board of Governors, and the Federal Open Market Committee), the Fed has expanded beyond its original mandate. Consider the second and third roles: to implement monetary policy by buying and selling US Treasury bonds and to maintain a strong payments system.

Today, the Fed certainly implements monetary policy. The Fed controls interest rates as a means of determining the value of the dollar and—in spite of the rather restrictive original definition of how the Fed was to implement policies—it does much more today than buy and sell Treasury bonds. A "strong payments system" may have had a relatively restrictive meaning in 1913, and we have to wonder what members of Congress would have thought about the original bill if they could see our economy today. Given the widespread isolationist view in that period, it is doubtful that Congress would have been willing to give over the power to the Fed to influence currency exchange values throughout the world. It would have been interesting to see how differently US monetary policy would have developed if the original bill had also tied the Fed's actions into a requirement that the United States remain on the gold standard. Alas, history is moved by conundrums. The dollar just happens to be one of the biggest, most challenging conundrums in financial history. And just happens to have come on our watch.

What is *real* money, then, in an inflationary period? This question should be on the minds of every investor and everyone who observes what happens at home and abroad. The US government has done an excellent job of convincing us that all of those dollar bills being exchanged work as actual money. In fact, though, everyone knows they have no tangible value. They are backed only by (1) a promise by the government to honor the debt and (2) assurances from the government that the money does have value, that one dollar is worth one dollar.

Both of these promises are questionable. How can the government promise to pay its debts when the total of that debt keeps getting higher and higher? It's already out of control. And in our fiat money system, the implied promise that a dollar is worth a dollar has to be looked at with suspicion as well.

This is not just an exercise in economic theory. The near future could prove to be a financial disaster for anyone who continues to have faith in the strength of the dollar. In fact, a collapse is inevitable, and it's only a question of how quickly it is going to occur.

The consequences will be huge declines in the stock market, savings becoming worthless, and the bond market completely falling apart. As the value of the dollar falls, that dollar will no longer be worth a dollar; it will be worth only pennies on the dollar. It will be a rude awakening for everyone who has become complacent about America's invulnerability.

The monster lurking in the near future has been caused by government policy. Our leaders have allowed foreign interests to take control of our economic destiny, and we cannot necessarily count those foreign interests as allies. We are not threatened by imminent invasion or loss of freedom to move about, but the extravagant American standard of living is about to be changed, drastically and suddenly. This has come about by three changes in fiscal status. First, the strength of the dollar and the level of interest rates are no longer in the control of the Fed. Second, good jobs have been sent overseas, and the so-called recovery has consisted of low-paying jobs. Third, because average wages are falling, Americans cannot afford inflation; even with our increasing credit card and mortgage–based bubble economy, the illusion of prosperity cannot go on forever.

HOW TO LOSE CONTROL OVER THE VALUE OF YOUR MONEY

The Fed has decided that nothing can ever stop the US economy. Continued growth is inevitable and—the ultimate delusion—our officials appear to truly believe that they can control it. If the economy slows, no problem. The Fed has declared lower and lower interest rates as a means for encouraging more and more debt—and that is called sound policy.

It's not just the consumer who has spent beyond his means. The government has led the way by bad example. US borrowing has expanded to the point that foreign central banks own major portions of the US debt. The Bank of Japan held $668 billion of Treasury securities in 2004, compared to the Federal Reserve holdings of $675 billion. In other words, the Bank of Japan nearly matched the Fed in ownership of US debt.[16] (Shortly after the first edition went to press, Japan began cutting its holdings, down to $582.2 billion as of September 2007—less than the debt the Fed owns, at $666.4 billion. If you just add in China, South Korea, and India, the Asian central banks own a lot more debt than the Fed does.)

With so many Asian currencies tied to the dollar, isn't it in their interests to keep dollar values high? Yes, but only to a point. Asian central banks will ultimately allow the US dollar to fall to contain inflation in their own countries. And the more debt those central banks control, the greater their control over the US dollar—and over the standard of living in the United States.

Should we fear global inflation? Again, we have to take into consideration the anomaly caused by the pandemic and the slowdown it caused in the Chinese economy, but it's worth noting that in 2022, China still had a growth rate greater than 3.6%.

Across the globe, in 2022, India, Saudi Arabia, Colombia, and the People's Republic of Congo all had post-pandemic growth rates of 6% or more. Perhaps, not too surprisingly, Iraq topped the growth chart with a growth rate of 9.3%. Ireland was close behind with a 9% increase; Australia and the United Kingdome are both still growing above 3%.[17]

The US economy was shrinking for the better part of the year—averaging out at 1.6% and is still facing the prospect of a full-blown recession. With the exception of Japan, which is also struggling at 1.7%, my point is real GDP growth in these countries is two and three times ours in the United States. The Fed's attempt to grapple with inflation has additional headwinds.

Ultimately, growth trends lead to inflation. The best way to fight inflation is to let your domestic currency grow in value. And here is where large holdings of US debt become important. Because central banks around the world hold vast sums of US debt, they can also directly impact the value of the dollar.

We are now seeing a trend in Asia toward buying fewer US dollars and then selling the holdings they already have, as well as selling off US bonds. All of these changes will force the US dollar to fall and interest rates to rise here at home. In other words, Asian inflation is held in check and transferred into US inflation. This will ultimately be the price the United States will have to pay for allowing its federal and consumer debt to get out of control.

So domestic interest rates are not really controlled by the Fed any longer. The fact that Asian central banks own such vast dollar reserves and hold so much debt means *they* will determine not only how much inflation takes place, but also *where* it takes place.

The trend toward dumping dollars and debt will have a direct impact on the US stock market. Because the dollar has been falling in recent years, foreign investors in US stocks—representing more than 10% of the whole market—have been getting lower returns on their investments. When the dollar takes an even sharper turn south, those foreign investors will sell. That will mean that the supply of stocks will increase rapidly or, putting it another way, prices will plummet as foreign investors start dumping US shares.

WHEN JOBS WERE SENT OVERSEAS

The US government likes to minimize the trend in outsourcing of jobs. They point to job numbers—the creation of millions of new jobs, especially in election years. But the sobering truth is far different.

The US labor market has traditionally been defined by higher wages than in any other industrialized country. But the emergence of cheap production overseas means that companies are going to seek the most competitive labor source. Therefore, high-paying jobs in the United States are disappearing, and rapidly. The average American factory worker gets $17.42 per hour, which works out to be around $36,230 a year.[18] In China, while wage rates vary by region, the average salary is still just $3.80, roughly $8,248 a year. You can see the difference. With US workers earning more in four months than Chinese laborers get in one year, our labor economy still cannot compete. The Chinese economy—with millions of people looking for work—can afford to compete with US wage levels by offering dirt-cheap pay, and there is an infinite supply glad for the work—even despite Chinese government complaints that wage rates are rising too quickly. The pandemic lockdowns have only made this situation more complicated.

As a consequence of globalization, wages in the United States are flat. In fact, for the first time in decades, wages actually fell in the United States in 2022, by more than 1%.[19] Of course, some isolated and highly specialized industries will continue to hold the edge in America, but on average, high-paying wages are being replaced overseas and our so-called job growth is in the lowest-paying industries. We see evidence everywhere. Almost no denim jeans are made in the United States anymore. Most of our clothing (95% of all footwear, for example) is imported from China and other Asian countries. More than half of all laptop computers are manufactured in Asia, and less than a decade ago virtually all of these were made in the United States.

What has brought about this huge change? We have to realize that the change is significant and has ramifications as great as any economic revolution. We must confront the fact that

> as a result of the breakdown of communist and socialist ideology and the end of isolationist policies on the Indian subcontinent—the world's economic sphere was enormously enlarged with close to three billion people joining our free-market, capitalistic system. The importance of adopting capitalism in countries like China, the former Soviet Union, Vietnam, and India cannot be underestimated and will again radically change global economic geography.[20]

Little discussion has been given on the impact of these three billion new capitalist competitors with the United States. It is, indeed, hard to fathom the overall impact of such a large shift in economic influence, but the shift is very real. The fact that US jobs are being transferred to countries that were previously in the Communist bloc makes the point: As long as these countries were our enemies, there was no trade between us. Now that we are all trading partners, all of those people are a cheap labor pool.

The problem goes back to the Fed and its ill-advised monetary policies. Driving down interest rates has, more than anything else, caused the shift in jobs. We want to buy from foreign countries, and we're content to do so with debt, especially as long as interest rates are low. Unfortunately, this has created *real* inflation throughout our economy, at least on the cost side. But on the wage side, we've seen no growth at all. And eventually, this disparity is going to backfire on the Fed and on the American consumer.

HIDDEN INFLATION IGNORES THE REALITY

With wages flat and prices starting to rise, something has to give. It's going to come to a head. Gas prices are increasing rapidly, cutting into the discretionary income of most American consumers. Think about where this is going to hurt the most. Three areas deserve special mention: gas prices, mortgages, and credit card debt.

1. *Gas prices.* That fill-up costing $17 or $18 only a few years ago has risen to $30 or $40 per tankful, and likely will go far higher before it settles down—above $100 a tank if you drive a monster SUV with a 30-gallon tank. That's a real bite out of anyone's budget. At the same time, with wages remaining flat and the dollar's buying power falling, the increased cost is even greater than the dollar-to-dollar comparison.
2. *Adjustable-rate mortgages.* More and more refinanced mortgages and first-time mortgages have been underwritten with dirt-cheap adjustable-rate mortgages. Even with annual caps on increases and life caps on the loans, many homeowners will not be able to keep up with their mortgage payments as higher rates begin to kick in. Remember, wages are flat, but interest expenses are going to rise. So as previous factory workers' hourly wages fall from $17 down to $10, mortgage lenders will be sending out letters telling them their monthly payments are going up.
3. *Credit card debt.* As people move debt around from one card to another with overall balances growing month after month,

it is possible to take advantage of low rates and special offers. These three-month no-interest or low-interest deals were great in the past because they allowed consumers to use so-called free money, at least for a few months. But what happens when those special deals start to disappear? Rates will rise, minimum payment levels will follow, and the free money will dry up. Credit card consumers will need to stop buying and to begin repaying their debt—at higher interest rates and using dollars of lower value.

It was only during the Powell Fed that the media gave up parroting the idea that while the dollar is falling against other currencies, we have little or no inflation. Yet a devalued dollar is precisely the definition of inflation in one sense. But inflation can be defined in another way too: Dollar values remain steady, but prices rise. In reality, these are just different aspects of the same phenomenon: a reduction in purchasing power.

Every investor will naturally want to look for ways to protect assets in the coming changes we are going to see. But those who understand the problem will also recognize that there is a solution. It is going to be found in the recognition of a single reality:

As the value of the dollar begins to fall, a corresponding and offsetting rise in value of commodities, raw materials, and tangible goods will occur.

In the large view, this means that investors will do best in the coming fall of the dollar by looking for investments that will benefit from that trend. For those who want to remain in the mutual fund sector, several funds emphasize profits resulting when the dollar falls and commodities (such as gold) rise in value. In the next section, you will see how open-end funds, closed-end funds, and exchange-traded funds (ETFs) can be used defensively to create profits when the dollar falls. The fund approach can work equally well to take advantage of rising prices in oil and other commodities.

For the sophisticated investor willing to take greater risks, currency speculation and using options or financial futures can be highly profitable. But these specialized derivatives markets demand great skill and experience, not to mention superb timing.

THE ESSENTIAL INVESTOR

The US economy is vulnerable on so many fronts. Social emphasis is being placed on protecting ourselves against terrorists and the threats of nuclear and chemical attack. But perhaps an equally serious peril is being ignored: our dependence on Middle East oil, for example.

We face a shrinking dollar, growing federal debt, increasing trade gap, record-high consumer debt, mortgage bubble, rising oil prices, inflation, flat productivity, falling wages—all part of the same trend translating to financial vulnerability, of course. But this economic sword of Damocles[21] points the way to how everyone can change their investing mode, not only to avoid loss but to *maximize* their investment profits.

If you accept the suggestion that big changes are going to be coming in these arenas, how can you reposition assets without also increasing market risks? Most investors are not going to sell their equity positions and go short on stocks, sell options, or sell futures. It simply isn't within their profile to do so. The trick is to find ways to take advantage of the coming changes in smart ways, and there are several. The way you choose to change strategies should depend on your investing experience and knowledge, risk tolerance, and personal preferences. In seeking ways to reposition your portfolio, keep in mind three major markets as places where you will want to either seek long positions: oil and natural gas, foreign investments, and gold. We still regard cryptocurrencies, options, green, and bio tech plays as speculative, unless you really know what you're doing.

Oil

Consistent with the inflationary period from 1971 to 1980, oil went from a low of $23.91 in 1973 to a high of $144.73 in 1980—a 526% increase in just seven years. One hundred and forty-four dollars in 1980 would be the equivalent of oil costing $518 today. After 1980, just like the gold price, gold took a two decade tumble down to a 1998 low of $20.31. And like the gold price, oil also bounced off the multi-decade low, climbing for the next 10 years to a fresh high of $189.84 in the height of the Panic of '08.

As you can see in Figure 8.3, after the high in May 2008, the price took a nosedive down $58.60 by December of the same year. These

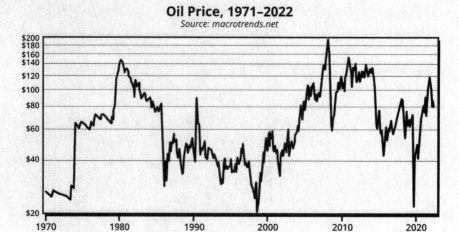

FIGURE 8.3 History of Oil Prices, 1971–2022
Source: macrotrends

are the kind of rapid moves both up and that make investing in ant-acids a viable consideration. For the next decade, while the Fed was keeping rates close to zero, oil traded in a range both above and below $60. It wasn't until the deep shock of March 2020 that oil dropped to $21.82, only to spike back up.

A year later, the Russian invasion of Ukraine, subsequent economic sanctions, and supply chain disruptions caused by the pandemic saw oil above $100 again. It hit $116.39 in May 2022. Like gold, oil is priced in dollars, so the sustained trend in oil is determined as much by dollar weakness as in short-term supply concerns. Russia has been trying to form alliances outside the dollar-dependent West, pricing its oil in rubles and seeking stronger relationships with India and China.[22]

Prior to the lockdowns, the oil price was also increasingly influenced by growing demand for oil from China. Our long-time allies in the oil markets have begun treaties selling oil directly to the Chinese priced in Yuan. Its oil imports were up nearly 40% in the early part of the twenty-first century. Since oil trades in a global market growing demand also driving up prices paid in the United States. Pre-pandemic, Chinese industry demand for oil was experiencing the highest growth curve in the world. We expect once the virus is dealt with to the Chinese government's satisfaction, consumption growth will return.

On its recent historical trend, COVID-19 notwithstanding, oil consumption in China, projected forward only a few years, has the capacity to outpace any hopes of production keeping up. We can safely assume based on the trend in both industrial and consumer use that China is going to be the major oil consumer in coming years. So there is no logical reason to expect oil prices to drop. Rising oil prices affect one-third of all US companies in some way. They create a double whammy on corporate profits. First, they drive up operating costs, and second, higher prices lead to reduced consumer spending. So it isn't just oil; it's the whole economy and any industry using petrochemicals, which includes construction, manufacturing, clothing, carpeting, and a vast number of other industries.

Increased demand affects oil prices as much as weather patterns, political problems, and of course the threat of terrorism. And there is little the United States can do to fix the problem. The relationship between oil discovery and production also looks quite dismal. With the current push toward green energy and a difficult regulatory environment in the United States for new drilling, transportation, or pipeline development, the headwinds are getting stronger.

What can investors do to position their portfolios? Stocks in companies involved in oil drilling and exploration, as well as those supplying drilling ventures, will continue to be solid investment opportunities in the future. New demand for oil rigs and drilling will push profits and stock prices higher. With OPEC already producing at 95% capacity, it is hollow to blame OPEC's policies for shortages. The truth is, reserves are dwindling as demand grows. Evaluate the oil production and drilling industry. Look for stocks that will benefit as oil prices rise. For mutual fund investors, seek out energy and commodity funds. For the more advanced investor who is comfortable with options, consider buying long-term calls in oil-related sectors with the greatest growth potential. Consider the four major subsectors within the larger energy sector of the market: coal, oil and gas (integrated), oil and gas operations, and oil well services and equipment.

Of course, looking for energy-related mutual funds and ETFs is also a wise move. With prices rising, oil and gas companies and their products will become more in demand in the future.

Foreign Investments

Why invest overseas? Let's recall that China holds a huge amount of US Treasury debt—not because it wants to per se but because holding US debt gives China economic leverage over the United States in several ways. First, it ensures the continued trade gap favoring China and hurting the US economy. Second, holding this debt enables China to virtually control US buying patterns, interest rates, and economic policy. Third, China's currency is largely pegged to the US dollar. If the dollar falls, so goes the yuan.

The more we buy from China, the more US debt China acquires. This helps its producing economy while further damaging our consumer economy. What happens next? In the summer of 2007, China began selling off US debt. This caused US interest rates to rise as the Treasury was forced to find new lenders. For those investors anticipating this change, several smart moves are available. Three potential strategies offset the consequences of US–China trade.

First, invest outside of the United States, either directly buying stocks or through ETFs. Seek investments in countries producing commodities and providing valuable resources, such as Australia. This continent is resource rich and geographically positioned to become a major supplier to China. Investing in Australia is a smart way to profit from China's growth without having to invest money in China itself.

Second, buy commodities by purchasing shares in corporations, index funds, or mutual funds specializing in the energy and commodities sector (oil and gas, precious metals, steelmaking). Third, use options to control large numbers of shares rather than buying shares directly.

The ultimate dollar hedge investment will always be gold. Investing in gold through ownership of the metal itself, mutual funds, or gold mining stock provides the most direct counter to the dollar. As the dollar falls, gold will inevitably rise.

In a moment, we'll provide you with many ways for positioning your portfolio to profit from a bull market in gold. For now, we emphasize the high probability of gold's future. The real potential for profits in the coming years and decades is not going to be found in the traditional American blue-chip industry. That is a financial dinosaur that can no longer compete in the world market. The future growth is going to be seen in gold. The world economy may remain off the gold standard, but ultimately the tangible value of gold as the basis for real value—whether acknowledged by central banks or not—will never change. Historically, this has always been the case, and it always will be. In other words, we are on a "gold standard" in spite of the popularity of fiat monetary systems.

Besides knowing where to position your capital to maximize returns when the dollar falls, also think about strategies that sell the dollar to produce profits.

How to Sell the Dollar

In 2004, then-Treasury Secretary John Snow was traipsing about the globe trying to "talk the dollar down." Why? In a word: debt. At the first writing of *Demise of the Dollar*, our debt stood at $7 trillion, with interest payments in fiscal 2003 totaling $318 billion. Now, the national debt is $31 trillion with paid interest of $3.6 trillion.[23,24]

The Fed and Treasury have engineered a strategy to pay off the debt with weaker and weaker dollars. And guess what? So far, so good. Of course, this is not the first time we've gone through a managed devaluation of the currency. In the 34-year period since Nixon slammed the gold window shut and subsequently ended the Bretton Woods exchange rate mechanism, we've had only six major currency trends:

1. Weak dollar 1972–1978 (7 years)
2. Strong dollar 1979–1985 (7 years)
3. Weak dollar 1986–1995 (10 years)
4. Strong dollar 1996–2001 (6 years)
5. Weak dollar 2002– 2008 (6 years)
6. Strong dollar 2011–2022 (11 years)

Until this latest run between 2011–2022, the most notable period spanned the 10 years from 1986 through 1995. After a historic run of growing strength against other foreign currencies, it's a good bet the dollar will have an extended weakening period of six or seven years. There are ways to play these big trends in the market—direct and indirect speculations, using short- and long-term options for each. These plays will help you safely position your money outside the dollar bear market. And you stand to make a fair amount of money, too.

But, as always, there is danger ahead. Once, we noted early in the last downtrend, the trade deficit passed the $759 billion mark—6.3% of GDP—foreigners had to shell out about $1.5 billion a day just to keep the dollar afloat. And even during the managed dollar decline of 2003, the trade imbalance continued to grow. In 2005, Stephen Roach, Morgan Stanley's chief global strategist, predicted that the current account deficit at the time was on course to reach $710 billion—6.5% of GDP. He was short by only a few billion.

Herein lies the drama. The Bank of Japan spent the equivalent of $187 billion in 2003—and $67 billion in January 2004 alone—in a bid to prevent its strengthening currency from choking off the country's export-led recovery. In dollar terms, the Bank of Japan is now spending more than $1.5 billion every day trying to keep the yen from strengthening against the greenback.

Over a four-week period in the fall of 2003, combined foreign central bank purchases of US securities topped $40 billion, more than $2 billion every trading day. Yet these central bank billions managed merely to limit the greenback's decline to just 2.3% over the same period. Can you imagine what would have happened if the banks hadn't pumped that money into the Fed's reserves? One former currency trader has asked, "If $40 billion cannot bring about even a minor rally, just how weak and despised is the once-almighty dollar?"[25]

We have had to rely on the kindness of strangers to keep the dollar afloat at all. And perhaps for far too long. "We're like the untrustworthy brother-in-law who keeps borrowing money, promising to pay it back, but can never seem to get out of debt," Jim Rogers writes. "Eventually, people cut that guy off."[26]

There is no way the United States can possibly pay off its creditors should they decide to cash in their IOUs. Right now, the United States holds only about $70 billion in reserves against its obligations—much less than 2005's $87 billion. That would last about three minutes should creditors begin to sell the dollar rather than trying to support it.

It's hard to imagine, isn't it? The world's reserve currency spiraling downward, out of control. But then, that's what the British must have thought in 1992 when they attempted to manage a devaluation of the pound. Despite the Bank of England's best efforts, sterling got away from them; the currency collapsed and Britain was kicked out of the Exchange Rate Mechanism (ERM) established to pave the way for the euro. On that day, known as Black Wednesday in Britain, currency speculator George Soros is rumored to have made as much as $2 billion. Don't be surprised if more fortunes emerge in the future as the dollar slips dangerously close to free fall.

By flooding the system with liquidity, the Fed cannot control the value of the US dollar against foreign currencies nor can the Fed control the dollar's purchasing power—at least not indefinitely. The Fed's current policies can "give the majority of investors the illusion of wealth as asset markets appreciate," wrote Marc Faber in November 2003,[27] "while the loss of the currency's purchasing power is hardly noticed. This is particularly true of a society that has a very large domestic market, where 90% of the people don't have a passport and therefore know little about what is going on outside their own continent. And where the import prices of manufactured goods are in continuous decline because of the entry of China, as a huge new supplier of products with an extremely low cost structure, into the global market economy." If that's the case, you should look at any declines in the dollar as an opportunity to make some money.

The dollar is the single biggest element of risk in the world of finance today. Rearrange the current system of world finance ever so slightly, let confidence in the greenback falter, and the mighty dollar could go up in flames. There are many ways to hedge against this risk. Better still, there are many ways to profit from the likelihood the dollar will fall. Some methods are direct, some indirect. Some are leveraged, some unleveraged. There is a methodology for every taste, but before explaining the specifics, we ask: What ails the dollar?

The dollar is a victim of its own success. It is America's most successful export ever—more successful than chewing gum, Levi's, Coca-Cola, or even Elvis Presley, Britney Spears, and Madonna put together. Trillions of dollars flow through the global financial markets every week, and they are readily accepted at large and small—and clandestine—business establishments from Kiev to Karachi.

Today, there are simply too many dollars in circulation for the currency's own good. Why? Americans have been living beyond their means for more than two decades. The US dollar's problems stem from a single cause. "If there's a bubble," wrote David Rosenberg, chief economist at Merrill Lynch, "it's in this four-letter word: debt. The US economy is just awash in it."[28]

You've seen it firsthand: John Q. Public now holds more credit cards and outstanding loans—with a higher and higher total debt load—than ever before. Outstanding consumer credit, including mortgage and other debt, reached $9.3 trillion in April 2003—a significant increase from its $7 trillion total in January 2000—but by the third quarter of 2007, debt had nearly doubled since 2000, to $13.7 trillion. With consumer spending alone responsible for approximately 70% of US GDP, that's quite a hefty personal debt load.

The corporate debt picture is no better. American companies have never depended so much on sales of their corporate bonds. Between 2002 and 2007, investment-grade corporate bond sales increased nearly 60%, growing from $598 billion to $951 billion. But junk bond sales for that same period broke the bank, surging from $57 billion to $133 billion.

The third leg of the debt problem, following consumer and business debt, is Uncle Sam. Government debt as of November 7, 2007, officially passed $9,000,000,000,000. That's about $30,000 for every man, woman, and child in the country. This total includes debt owned by many types of investors, from individuals to corporations to Federal Reserve banks and especially to foreign interests. (By 2004, foreign central banks had stockpiled more than $1.3 trillion worth of dollar-denominated Treasury bonds and agency bonds at the Federal Reserve. By 2007, foreign debt had nearly doubled, to $2.033 trillion.) What the $7.8 trillion figure does not account for are items like the gap between the government's Social Security and Medicare commitments and the money put aside to pay for them. If these items are factored in, the government debt burden for every American rises to well over $175,000.

If we're nearing the end of an 11-year stretch of a strengthening dollar, what should you do? On way to answer that question is look at what great investors have done.

In 2005, the Methuselah of investment mavens, Sir John Templeton, then 93, said you should get out of US stocks, the US dollar, and excess residential real estate. Templeton believed the dollar would fall 40% against other major currencies, and that this would lead the nation's major creditors—notably Japan and China—to dump their US bonds, which would cause interest rates to run up, thus beginning a long period of stagflation. He was right.

Don't let his age fool you—Templeton was still sharp in 1999 when the financial industry hacks in Florida were urging their customers to buy more tech stocks. Templeton warned that the bubble would soon burst. He was right; they were wrong. Of course, he was only 87 back then. Templeton died in 2008 at the age of 96. He didn't live long enough to see what he was confident would be on the horizon. Were he alive today, he'd almost certainly be right again.

Other great investors were also getting out of the dollar. For the first time in his life, Warren Buffett was investing in foreign currencies. George Soros, who made a fortune selling sterling in the 1992 ERM crisis, warns that the US system could "blow up" at any time. Richard Russell, the influential editor of the *Dow Theory* letters, speaking at the New Orleans Investment Conference, warned: "If ever there was a crisis that could shake the global economy—this is it."

When old-timers nod their heads in agreement—especially when they happen to be the most successful investors in the world—their advice may be worth listening to. The trend they observed is likely coming around today, again.

American consumers, companies, the US government, and the country as a whole owe more dollars to more people than ever before. But perhaps the greatest threat to the US economy is its foreign creditors. There is a market-based limit to the number of dollars foreigners are willing to buy and hold and thus a limit to their willingness to service our credit habit. Why? Because the United States, while still the world's number-one economic power, is showing itself to be an erratic steward of its own currency.

You don't spend your way to prosperity; no nation ever has or ever will. But guess what? That very idea *is* the basis of US and Fed monetary policy. Never in US history have the imbalances in the economy been so pronounced, or so dangerous. "My experience as an emerging markets analyst in the 1990s taught me to be on the lookout for signs of financial vulnerability," observed analyst Hernando Cortina in a

Morgan Stanley research note in 2003. His words ring just as true today:

> [The signs] include ballooning current-account and fiscal deficits, overvalued currencies, dependence on foreign portfolio flows, optimistic stock market valuations coupled with murky earnings, questionable corporate governance, and acrimonious political landscapes. Any one of these signals in an emerging market usually raises a red flag, and a market that combines all of them is almost surely best avoided or at least underweighted. I didn't imagine back then that one day these indicators would all be flashing red for the world's biggest and most important market—the USA by-the-numbers analysis of America's macro accounts in a global context doesn't paint a flattering picture.[29]

Yet for growth-starved financial markets, perceptions and hope are often more important than economic reality. According to the macro indicators that the IMF uses to assess emerging-market economies, the United States fell between Turkey and Brazil. Hernando Cortina politely concluded: "Investors contemplating the purchase of US dollar-denominated assets would be wise to factor in significant dollar depreciation over the next few years."

"Households have been on a borrowing spree," added Northern Trust economist Asha Bangalore also in 2003. As we've seen, that trend is as apparent and true today, if worse. Consumer credit is skyrocketing while the savings rate has plummeted. Bangalore:

> This measure of household borrowing reflects mortgage borrowing, credit card borrowing, borrowing from banks, and the like. Household borrowing is not only at a record high but a new aspect has emerged—household borrowing advanced during the recession unlike in every other postwar recession when households reduced borrowing. The good news is that consumer demand continues to advance with the support from borrowing.[30]

The bad news is that no economy has ever borrowed its way to prosperity. Despite the conspiracy against it, the dollar has avoided a downright free fall. That's because dollar investors across the globe are still convinced that, given favorable credit conditions, the US economy will surely reenter the heyday of the late 1990s, taking dollar-denominated assets to new heights. But someday soon, we think, investors will be disabused of their illusions. Sure, the stock market rallied briskly in the recent past, but the US economy continues to struggle. Unemployment persists. And the twin deficits loom larger and larger.

If and when America's creditors—domestic and foreign—decide the country's massive, record-breaking level of debt is reason enough to get out of their dollar investments, the dollar will have nowhere to go but down, precipitously. We don't know when the exact moment of truth will arrive, but we know it cannot be far off.

Excessive debt is not the only ominous development in the US economy. Just as foreboding is the American consumers' persistent belief that they are wealthier than they actually are. US financial assets are, once again, in the grip of a large bubble, despite fears of a recession. The Fed's frantic attempt to fight inflation spooked stocks into bear market territory in 2022. But late in the year the market began a rally again in a way completely dissociated from any real measure of value.

In fact, the rally in stocks has been so strong that it has rekindled investors' belief in a new bull market, full economic recovery in the United States. But a funny thing has started to happen. The US stock market is soaring. Normally, that means the dollar would go with it; when a country's stock market goes up, demand for its financial assets usually goes up, too. But the dollar is beginning to get dragged down again by debt—government debt, personal debt, and corporate debt. Investors want a bull market, and so they're making one. But the dollar reflects the real state of the American economy . . . and it knows better.

Foreign investors are especially burned when stocks and the dollar part company. At first blush, the rallying US stock market seems like a very inviting place for their capital. All denominations are welcome, but not all guests are treated equally well.

Foreign bondholders are faring no better. US debt held by foreign countries is $7.07 trillion.[31] So, roughly speaking, every 10% drop in the dollar's value impoverishes our foreign creditors by about $100 billion on their US Treasury holdings alone!

That's real money. But if you look closely at the timer clicking away on US Debt.org, the dollar amount of debt held by foreigners is dropping almost as rapidly as the rate of spending is going up!

How is it possible that stocks continue their winning ways, even while the dollar continues its losing ways? These two inimical trends are strange bedfellows indeed. What makes the pairing particularly bizarre is the fact that our nation relies so heavily upon the enthusiasm of foreign investors for US assets.

What is the Fed doing, and why? One writer has pegged the answer:

> The Federal Reserve Board [manage] the inflation rate, while the US Treasury is trying to talk down the dollar exchange rate. Not every day does the world's hegemonic power pursue a policy of currency debasement. Still less frequently does it have the courtesy to tell its creditors what it's doing to them.[32]

Indeed. The Fed and Treasury are engaged in a kind of collusion to lower the dollar's value. And that's a very dangerous game to play, especially for a country like the United States, which relies so heavily upon foreign capital to finance its economy. It has become fashionable in the corridors of power in Washington to advocate "market-based" exchange rates—code for "weak dollar." A weak dollar, it is widely believed, will lead to a strong economy. Hmm.

In the olden days, of course, the Fed was supposed to pursue "monetary stability." But in the enlightened twenty-first century, the Fed has much grander designs. It imagines itself a kind of marionette master to the world's largest economy, making it dance whenever it wishes, simply by tugging on one little interest rate, or by tugging on the dollar. And so it tugs, and tugs, hoping to revive the economy.

The US Treasury Department is also conspiring with the Fed to weaken the dollar. Hasn't Treasury Secretary Snow touted the weak dollar as a surefire cure for the struggling US manufacturing sector? And hasn't the dollar been tumbling? And yet, isn't the manufacturing sector struggling just as much as it was when the price of a euro was only 83 cents, instead of $1.25?

It's obvious to almost every citizen who does not live in Washington, DC, that devaluing the dollar to stimulate economic growth is a fool's mission. At the turn of the century a little under three hundred dollar bills purchased an ounce of gold. Today, an ounce of gold costs 2,000 paper dollars. Our manufacturers will have become so competitive that they will be exporting firecrackers to the Chinese, or so the gang on Capitol Hill believes. But in fact, we will all be poorer for embracing the idiocy of "competitive devaluations." The problem is, once a devaluation trend begins—we call it inflation—it is very difficult to stop.

A TREND WHOSE PREMISE IS FALSE

"Find the trend whose premise is false, and bet against.

—George Soros

So what do you do now? The solution comes from repositioning, and the best cues for when, how, and where are found in the gold market—which prospers during times of geopolitical uncertainty and traditionally rises in value when the dollar falls. As we've noted, over the past two decades the spot price of gold has risen from $235 in 1999 to a sustained level around $2,000 by the early 2020s. The metal's impressive rise inspired a dramatic rally in gold shares that has vaulted the XAU Index of gold stocks to a high of $226 in 2011. By 2022, it was making another run starting the year at $158.

What does the gold market know? That the Fed's reflation campaign will succeed too well? A little bit of inflation—like a little wildfire—is a difficult thing to contain. And the gold market seems to have caught a whiff of inflationary smoke.

Or does the gold market know that Iraq will continue to serve as a breeding ground for terrorists and a habitat for anti-American terrorist acts? As the Iraq situation continues, the dollar will suffer . . . a lot.

Or maybe the gold market knows only that US financial assets are very expensive, and worries, therefore, that US stocks selling for 35 times earnings and US bonds yielding 4.5% are all too pricey for risk-averse investors to own in large quantities. A vicious cycle is hard to stop. The dollar's descent is the most worrisome—and influential—trend in the financial markets today. And yet, as long as Cisco is "breaking out to the upside," few investors seem to care about the dollar's slide into the dustbin of monetary history. The dollar's demise is not inevitable, just highly likely.

When a currency falls, in theory anyway, interest rates usually rise. A government whose currency is falling apart tries to make assets denominated in that currency more attractive by paying higher rates of interest to potential investors. And if the government doesn't raise rates, the market will do it by selling off bonds and driving yields up.

And so, in theory, you would normally expect to see a falling US dollar accompanied by rising US interest rates. The difficulty from the Bush/Greenspan/Bernanke perspective is that rising long-term rates pose an enormous problem: They make it significantly more expensive for debtors—from US consumers to the US government—to service their obligations. And these costs are not negligible.

In fiscal year 2007, for example, the government was obliged to pay out a whopping $429 billion in interest expense on the public debt outstanding. At a 1% rise in interest rates, that would add $43 billion in interest expense. And to meet this added interest expense, the government would, of course, have to float even more bonds, and at the higher interest rate.

This scenario is the government's nightmare. When the falling dollar eventually pushes interest rates up, the Treasury will have to issue more debt at higher interest rates simply to pay off its existing debt. But if the Asian economic juggernaut were to discontinue recycling its excess dollars into US government bonds and Fannie Mae debt, the dollar would suffer mightily. How much longer until our luck runs out?

In some way, shape, or form foreigners lend our consumption-crazed nation $1 trillion every year. We Americans, in turn, use the money they send our way to buy SUVs, plasma TVs, and costly military campaigns in distant lands. However, we do not forget to repay our creditors with ever-cheaper dollars. Someday soon, foreigners must lose interest in subsidizing our consumption habit.

That the dollar's decline comes at the urging of the same nation that prints the things is an irony that is not lost on the world's largest dollar holders. Reading the tea leaves, many Asian central banks are still exploring ways to lighten up on their US dollar holdings. "The Chinese aren't lapping up our Treasury paper for its great investment attributes," writes Stephanie Pomboy of MacroMavens, "but [rather] because of a mechanical need to maintain the yuan/dollar peg."[33]

The dollar's resistance to its debt load, fueled by the machinations of central banks and the misguided faith of dollar investors, undoubtedly qualifies as a trend whose premise is false. Sometime soon this trend will be discredited.

Fortunately, there are many ways you can capitalize on a falling dollar. From the wide range of possibilities, four investment strategies follow, each designed to suit a variety of investing styles. Using one or several of these recommendations, you can craft a personalized plan of action.

The most direct—albeit short-term—approach to betting against the dollar is to buy put options on Dollar Index futures. The US Dollar Index (USDX) trades on the New York Board of Trade under the symbol DX. The USDX was invented in 1973—ironically, two years after Nixon closed the gold window, and the same year the gold standard was completely abandoned. Using a base of 100, the USDX measures the market value of the dollar versus the trade-weighted geometric average of six currencies (although 17 countries are represented in the index because there are 15 countries that use the euro). The six currencies are the euro, the Japanese yen, the UK pound, the Canadian dollar, the Swedish krona, and the Swiss franc.

Why these countries and these currencies? These six currencies constitute most of America's international trade (excepting Mexico and China) and have relatively well-developed foreign exchange markets. Most important, the values of these currencies are, with the exception of central bank intervention, freely determined by market forces and market participants.

As you can see from the graph of the US Dollar Index in Figure 8.3, the greenback has been in decline against a basket of currencies since the beginning of 2002. It was hovering around the 87 level by late 2004. Given the dollar's continuing predicament, we can see nowhere for it to go but down.

Purchasing put options on the USDX is the most direct way to capitalize on the dollar's decline. By purchasing these options, you'll be paying the price—known as the premium—to have the right for a fixed period of time *but not the obligation* to be short the Dollar Index at a specific level. Should the dollar fail to fall, or should it even rally (highly unlikely), you would simply not exercise your right to be short the dollar—forfeiting the premium paid for the put option, but no more.

Consider buying US Dollar Index put options dated at least four months into the future, looking for the index to fall. Your maximum risk is the price you pay for your options plus transaction costs. Your profit potential is unlimited.

Buying euro call options is almost identical to buying puts on the USDX. If the dollar drops, the euro should rise. But whereas the USDX measures the greenback's value against a basket of foreign currencies, the euro is only one of the currencies in the USDX. Buying calls on the euro, therefore, is a more focused trade.

The euro boasts one very important virtue that the dollar lacks: a current account *surplus*. Because the euro bloc countries produce a current account surplus, there is an automatic, natural demand for euros. Conversely, America's large and growing current account deficit produces continuous selling pressure on the dollar.

Just as for the dollar puts, call options on euro currency futures are promising ways to sell the dollar. The euro index has been rising steadily since the dollar peaked in February of 2002. The futures market for euros will anticipate further upward movement, rewarding buyers of call options on the euro.

Consider buying Euro FX call options dated at least four months into the future. Your maximum risk is the price you pay for your options plus transaction costs. Your profit potential is unlimited.

For most investors, the surest way to profit from the weakening US dollar is to invest directly in strong currencies and their certificates of deposit (CDs). By investing directly in a strong currency, you reduce your risks considerably because you are dealing with a single investment that you own outright and can easily monitor. At the same time, you can be certain to receive whatever exchange-rate advantages may develop between your foreign currency and the weakening US dollar.

Until recently, opening a foreign currency account could be done only through an offshore bank. Many countries did not make it easy for their banks to deal with Americans. In addition, offshore bank accounts led to additional paperwork with the IRS and an increased chance for an audit. Fortunately for US investors, foreign currency accounts are now easily available.

All–Season Dollar Hedge: Gold

Gold is the ultimate dollar hedge. It is the only global currency that is no one's liability. It is "pure money." As such, gold has always provided a kind of insurance, first and foremost. It is not an investment per se. But when economic uncertainties mount, buying a bit of gold "insurance" can be a terrific investment.

"If gold isn't a bargain, what is it? It is a hedge," says Jim Grant, editor of *Grant's Interest Rate Observer*. "However, in my opinion, it is a hedge bargain. The value of a hedge should vary according to the cost and evidence of the risks being hedged against. In the case of gold, the risks are monetary."

The abandonment of the gold standard in 1971 was a crucial turning point in the US economy, a decision that has been gradually destroying the power of the United States. The excessive printing of currency led directly to the trade deficit, and once the surplus turned, it never went back. It aggravated the condition of the national debt and allowed the Fed unbridled access to printing presses, the condition in which we find ourselves today.

The lesson not yet learned has everything to do with the reasons why the gold standard was so important. We have given control of economic forces over to government tinkering. Ludwig von Mises, noted twentieth-century economist, was a believer in allowing market forces and not government to determine monetary policy:

> Mises argued that because money originated as a market commodity, not by government edict or social contract, it should be returned to the market. Banking should be treated as any other industry in a market economy, and be subject to competition.[34]

In one of his many writings, Mises correctly observed, "The significance of adherence to a metallic-money system lies in the freedom of the value of money from state influence that such a system guarantees."[35]

This is the crux of the monetary struggle of our era. With governments virtually off the gold standard, the market itself is not trusted to set the course of *value* in the exchange of goods and services. That is why, ultimately, the destruction of the dollar is inevitable. Governments—including the US government along with the Fed—have not yet learned that the economy cannot be controlled. But as Mises explained, it is not just monetary policy but part of a larger social trend that has brought us to this moment:

> The struggle against gold which is one of the main concerns of all contemporary governments must not be looked upon as an isolated phenomenon. It is but one item in the gigantic process of destruction which is the mark of our time. People fight the gold standard because they want to substitute national autarky for free trade, war for peace, totalitarian government omnipotence for liberty.[36]

If all of this is true—and from the economic news of the past few years, it appears so—what can you do to turn this situation into an advantage? The answer is to use free-market gold to exploit the market tendency of gold itself. Remember, even when governments are off the gold standard, the market for gold cannot be controlled. It is worth whatever people will pay. As long as you understand what causes the price of gold to move, you have the key to investing success. That key is:

The price of gold tends to move in a direction opposite the value of the dollar.

With this simple observation, we can track the value of gold and the value of the dollar together to see how they interact with one another. After 2000, the dollar fell, and gold prices rose. As the dollar continues to fall, it makes sense that gold will move upward in direct response. We could explain this by noting that value itself is not created out of nothing; it simply changes hands. So as value goes out of the dollar, it can be measured by watching other currencies rise, but it can also be measured by watching gold prices move in the other direction, opposite the dollar.

As the Fed continues to keep the printing presses running around the clock, the dollar continues to weaken. The problem is not entirely visible because, even with its gradual decline, the dollar has remained strong. This has been so partly because China's currency is largely pegged to the dollar, but also because in many respects, the United States continues to lead economically in the world. However, the trend in economic growth tells us that this cannot continue indefinitely. It is economic common sense that currencies tend to be the strongest for those nations with superior economic growth. If you understand why it is important to invest in gold as a defensive measure against the declining dollar, the next question is *where* to invest. You have many choices.

Five ways to invest in gold are explained in the following paragraphs. Based on your level of market experience and familiarity with products, one of these will be appropriate for you.

1. *Direct ownership.* There is nothing like gold bullion, the ultimate expression of pure value. Historically, many civilizations have recognized the permanence of gold's value. For example, Egyptian civilizations buried vast amounts of gold with deceased pharaohs in the belief that they would be able to use it in the afterlife. Great wars were fought, among other reasons, to pillage stores of gold. Why the allure? The answer: Gold is the only *real* money, and its value cannot be changed or controlled by government fiat—the underlying reason for governments to go off the gold standard, unfortunately. Gold's value will rise based on the pure forces of supply and demand, no matter what Bernanke decrees regarding interest rates or greenbacks in circulation.

   The big disadvantage to owning gold is that it tends to trade with a wide spread between bid and ask prices. So don't expect to turn a fast profit. You'll buy at retail and sell at wholesale, so you'll need a big price jump just to break even. However, you should not view gold as a speculative asset, but a defensive asset for holding value. Since your dollars are going to fall in value, gold is the best place to preserve value. The best forms for gold ownership are through minted coins: one-ounce South African Krugerrands, Canadian Maple Leafs, or American Eagles.

2. *Gold exchange-traded funds.* The recent explosion in ETFs presents an even more interesting way to invest in gold. An ETF is a type of mutual fund that trades on a stock exchange like an ordinary stock. The ETF's exact portfolio is fixed in

advance and does not change. Thus, the two gold ETFs that trade in the United States both hold gold bullion as their one and only asset. You can locate these two ETFs under the symbol "GLD" (for the streetTRACKS Gold Trust) and "IAU" (for the iShares COMEX Gold Trust). Either ETF offers a practical way to hold gold in an investment portfolio.

3. *Gold mutual funds.* For people who are hesitant to invest in physical gold, but still desire some exposure to the precious metal, gold mutual funds provide a helpful alternative. These funds hold portfolios of gold stocks—that is, the stocks of companies like Newmont Mining that mine for gold. Newmont is an example of a senior gold stock.

   A senior is a large, well-capitalized company that has been around several years and has a profitable track record. They tend to own established mines that produce known quantities of gold each year. For many investors, selection of such a company is a more moderate or conservative play (versus picking up cheap shares in fairly young companies).

4. *Junior gold stocks.* This level of stock is more speculative. Junior stocks are less likely to own productive mines and may be exploration plays—with higher potential profits but also with greater risk of loss. Capitalization is likely to be smaller than capitalization of the senior gold stocks. This range of investments is for investors whose risk tolerance is broader and who accept the possibility of gold-based losses in exchange for the potential for triple-digit gains.

5. *Gold options and futures.* For the more sophisticated and experienced investor, options allow you to speculate on gold prices. In the options market, you can speculate on price movements in either direction. If you buy a call, you are hoping prices will rise. A call fixes the purchase price so the higher that price goes, the greater the margin between your fixed option price and current market price. When you buy a put, you expect the price to fall. Buying options is risky, and more people lose than win. In fact, about three-fourths of all options bought expire worthless. The options market is complex and requires experience and understanding.

To generalize, options possess two key traits—one bad and one good. The good trait is that they enable an investor to control a large investment with a small, and limited, amount of money. The bad trait is that options expire within a fixed period of time. Thus, for the buyer time is the enemy because as the expiration date gets closer, an option's time value disappears. Anyone investing in options needs to understand all of the risks before spending money.

The futures market is far too complex for the vast majority of investors. Even experienced options investors recognize the high-risk nature of the futures market. Considering the range of ways to get into the gold market, futures trading is the most complex, and while big fortunes could be made, they can also be lost in an instant.

We cannot know, predict, or even guess *when* the demise of the dollar is going to occur or how quickly it will take place. But as we've demonstrated, fiat currencies don't last long. The tragic mismanagement of monetary policy by the Fed over many years has made this inevitable.

Removing the US monetary system from the gold standard was not merely a decision of short-term effect. Nixon may have seen the move as a means for solving current economic problems, but it had long-lasting impacts: trade deficits, growing federal debt, and the ability to print money endlessly and build a new credit-based economy. Internationally, the decision by the United States virtually forced all other major currencies to also go off the gold standard.

Any investor who views the economic situation broadly—both domestically and internationally—can see that trouble lies ahead. We have delayed the inevitable because China is a partner in our monetary woes. The Chinese are building their own debt on the dubious foundation of the US dollar, and other Asian economies have been forced to go along for the ride. When the dollar falls, many other countries will suffer as well. The offset, logically, is found in commodities. Investing in oil stocks makes sense, for example, because the price of oil is rising, and as it becomes more difficult to drill, those companies that own drilling and exploration operations will benefit.

It makes sense to invest in other commodities as well. The *tangible* asset play is clearly where future value is going to lie. With China's never-ending need for coal, iron ore, tungsten, copper, oil, and other metals, the future of tangible markets is the bright spot in the gloomy financially based economics of the world.

Leading the charge is gold. It is ironic that monetary policy follows a predictable pattern. Governments overprint money, and their currency crashes. Inevitably, they always return to gold, but often at great expense and with considerable suffering. We find ourselves in another one of those moments in time where irresponsible monetary policy has put us at risk. But we don't have to simply hold on and wait for the demise of the dollar; we can take action now because that demise *is* great for your portfolio—if you position yourself in tangible assets rather than in empty fiat promises and the bizarre economic premise of US monetary policy.

Remember the observation we made earlier: Goods and services can be paid for only with goods and services. Currency is nothing but an IOU, a promissory note that is *not* backed up with any tangible value. Once we reach our national credit limit, monetary policy will be forced to retreat. When that happens, traditional investors and their savings accounts are going to be hit hard. The beneficiary of the falling dollar will be the investor whose holdings emphasize tangible value of goods: resources and precious metals.

Every danger to one group of people is invariably an opportunity to another. It all depends on where you position yourself. Those investors positioned in dollar-based investments are going to suffer the loss of purchasing power when the dollar's value disappears. Those who moved their investments to higher ground will benefit from the change.

NOTES

CHAPTER 1: THE GREENBACK BOOGIE

1. "Harry Dexter White." 2023. Wikipedia. January 12, 2023. https://en.wikipedia.org/wiki/Harry_Dexter_White#:~:text=Through%20Bretton%20Woods%2C%20White%20was.
2. Money Matters, an IMF Exhibit -- the Importance of Global Cooperation, Destruction and Reconstruction (1945-1958), Part 1 of 6." n.d. Www.imf .org. Accessed January 25, 2023.https://www.imf.org/external/np/exr/center/mm/eng/mm_dr_01.htm#:~:text=By%201947%2C%20the%20United%20States,to%20pay%20for%20the%20war.
3. Cited in Francis J. Gavin, *Gold, Dollars and Power: The Politics of International Monetary Relations, 1958–1971* (Chapel Hill: University of North Carolina Press, 2003).

CHAPTER 2: "WE ARE ALL KEYNESIANS NOW"

1. "Return to Bretton Woods." 2023. Guggenheimpartners.com. 2023. https://www.guggenheimpartners.com/perspectives/global-cio-outlook/return-to-bretton-woods#:~:text=Between%20Bretton%20Woods'%20establishment%20in,reserves%20in%20a%20short%20time.

2. "Money: De Gaulle v. the Dollar." 1965. Time.com. https://content.time.com/time/subscriber/article/0,33009,840572-2,00.html.
3. Emergency Banking Relief Act of 1933.
4. Strange to note that if price controls didn't work in the 1970s, why did "the West" try to impose price controls on Russian oil in early December 2022? Some things we learn by experience. When it comes to politics and public persuasion, logic goes out the window entirely.

CHAPTER 3: ATTENTION TO DEFICITS DISORDER

1. H. A. Scott Trask, "Perpetual Debt: From the British Empire to the American Hegamon," at www.mises.org, January 27, 2004.
2. Ibid.
3. "$37 in 1809 → 2023 | Inflation Calculator." n.d. Www.officialdata.org. Accessed January 17, 2023. https://www.officialdata.org/us/inflation/1809?amount=37
4. H. A. Scott Trask, "Perpetual Debt: From the British Empire to the American Hegamon," at www.mises.org, January 27, 2004.
5. We had used Government Accounting Office numbers in 2006–2008 while filming our documentary, *I.O.U.S.A* and thought we were being alarmists when we predicted $10 trillion in national debt. When we premiered the film on August 22, 2008, the national debt was $9 trillion. Six weeks later Lehman Brothers went bankrupt. The bailout period began overnight and by September 30, 2008—the nation's fiscal year-end—the debt had already passed $10 trillion. Less than four months later, by the time Barack Obama was sworn into office, the debt had crossed $11 trillion. If you're interested in some morbid entertainment check out the whirring pace at which the national debt is increasing at https://www.usdebtclock.org/.
6. David Walker, Letter, "Report to the Secretary of the Treasury," Financial Audit, Bureau of the Public Debt's Fiscal Years 2007 and 2006 Schedules of Federal Debt, November 2007.
7. Jon Dougherty, "Is the United States Flat-Out Broke?" *World Net - Daily*, June 6, 2003.
8. Hans F. Sennholz, "The Surplus Hoax," at www.mises.org, November 3, 2000.
9. www.cbo.gov.
10. "Debt Limit." n.d. U.S. Department of the Treasury. https://home.treasury.gov/policy-issues/financial-markets-financial-institutions-and-fiscal-service/debt-limit#:~:text=Since%201960%2C%20Congress%20has%20acted,29%20times%20under%20Democratic%20presidents.
11. In *The Birds* (play by Aristophanes, ca. 415 B.C.), Cloud Cuckoo Land was a utopian land existing in the air between heaven and earth, where everything was perfect and all problems solved themselves.

12. Cited in Murray N. Rothbard, "Repudiating the National Debt," at www
    .mises.org, January 16, 2004.
13. "Major Foreign Holders of U.S. Treasury Securities 2022." n.d. Statista.
    https://www.statista.com/statistics/246420/major-foreign-holders-of-us-
    treasury-debt.
14. Adam Smith, *The Wealth of Nations,* 1776.
15. "A national debt, if it is not excessive, will be to us a national blessing."
    —Alexander Hamilton, in a letter dated April 30, 1781.
16. Joseph Kennedy II, quoted in *Newsweek,* February 9, 1967.
17. Joint Economic Committee, United States Congress: "Deficits, Taxation,
    and Spending," April 2003; and "Hidden Costs of Government Spending,"
    staff report, 2001.
18. Joint Economic Committee, "Deficits, Taxation, and Spending."
19. Joint Economic Committee, United States Congress: James Gwartney,
    Robert Lawson, and Randall Holcombe, "The Size and Functions of
    Government and Economic Growth," 1998.
20. Senator John C. Calhoun (Democratic-Republican Party, South Carolina),
    speech, August 5, 1842.
21. Gerald W. Scully, "Measuring the Burden of High Taxes," Policy Report
    No. 215, National Center for Policy Analysis, July 1998.
22. "Debt Limit." n.d. U.S. Department of the Treasury. Accessed January 25,
    2023. https://home.treasury.gov/policy-issues/financial-markets-financial-
    institutions-and-fiscal-service/debt-limit#:~:text=Since%201960%2C%20
    Congress%20has%20acted,29%20times%20under%20Democratic%20
    presidents.
23. International Monetary Fund, "Global Financial Market Developments."
24. Peter Warburton, *Debt and Delusion: Central Bank Follies That Threaten
    Economic Disaster,* 2nd ed. (London: Penguin Books, 2000).
25. Alan Greenspan, testimony before the Committee on Banking, Housing,
    and Urban Affairs, February 17, 2005.
26. "FTX Crash: Timeline, Fallout and What Investors Should Know." n.d.
    NerdWallet. https://www.nerdwallet.com/article/investing/ftx-crash.
27. "46 Quotes on Inflation & Rising Prices (HIDDEN TAX)." 2022. Gracious
    Quotes. September 20, 2022. https://graciousquotes.com/inflation.

CHAPTER 4: HERE COMES THE BOOM

1. "Personal Saving Rate | U.S. Bureau of Economic Analysis (BEA)." 2019.
   Bea.gov. 2019. https://www.bea.gov/data/income-saving/personal-saving-rate.
2. "Consumer Price Index Unchanged over the Month, up 8.5 Percent over
   the Year, in July 2022: The Economics Daily: U.S. Bureau of Labor Statistics."
   n.d. Www.bls.gov. Accessed January 17, 2023. https://www.bls.gov/opub/

ted/2022/consumer-price-index-unchanged-over-the-month-up-8-5-
percent-over-the-year-in-july-2022.htm#:~:text=Consumer%20Price%20
Index%20unchanged%20over,U.S.%20Bureau%20of%20Labor%20Statistics.

3. This section is based on Dr. Kurt Richebächer's "The Austrian Case against American Monetarism," *The Daily Reckoning,* June 7, 2000.

4. www.oecd.org.

5. We began hoping our government officials were paying attention with the publication of the first edition of *Financial Reckoning Day* in 2002. Twenty years later it appears they have been paying attention all along. They're following in lockstep!

6. Shinzo Abe, the prime minister of Japan from 2006 to 2007 and again from 2012 to 2020, pioneered a government spending pattern since named after him: Abenomics. Abe was the longest serving prime minister in Japan's history. He was assassinated while speaking at a political event near Nara City, Japan. The assailant shot Abe in the back with a homemade gun. Without getting too deep in the woods on Abe's politics or economic ideas, it's safe to say he wasn't popular with at least one person. Abe was trying to deal with the exact economic and financial scenario in Japan that the United States faces today: an aging population with limited resources and a stock market more interested in short term gain than planning for the future.

7. *BusinessWeek Online,* 2002 S&P Core Earnings table.

8. Janice Revell, "CEO Pensions: The Latest Way to Hide Millions," *Fortune,* April 28, 2003.

9. John C. Edmunds, "Securities: The New World Wealth Machine," *Foreign Policy,* Fall 1996, at www.foreignpolicy.com.

10. The Institute for Supply Management publishes the index as a means for monitoring trends in the industry. Web site: www.ism.ws/AboutISM/index.cfm.

11. See "Haute Con Job," PIMCO *Investment Outlook,* October 2004.

12. The G-5 nations are the United States, United Kingdom, France, Germany, and Japan.

13. Ben S. Bernanke, "National and Regional Economic Overview," Charlotte Chamber of Commerce, Charlotte, North Carolina, November 29, 2007.

14. Ibid.

15. Krishna Guha and Daniel Pimlot, "Bernanke Clears Way for Fed Rate Cut," *Financial Times,* November 29, 2007. https://www.ft.com/content/86516d38-9e92-11dc-b4e4-0000779fd2ac.

16. Ben S. Bernanke, "National and Regional Economic Overview," Charlotte Chamber of Commerce, Charlotte, North Carolina, November 29, 2007.

17. James A. Dorn, *Reflections on Greenspan's "Irrational Exuberance" Speech After 25 Years.* Cato at Liberty, December 27, 2021. https://www.cato.org/blog/reflections-greenspans-irrational-exuberance-speech-after-25-years#:~:text=On%20December%205%2C%201996%2C%20Alan,he%20coined%20the%20term%20%E2%80%9Cirrational.

18. "The Economy on the Edge," Bloomberg, November 19, 2007. https://www.bloomberg.com/news/articles/2007-11-18/the-economy-on-the-edge#xj4y7vzkg.

CHAPTER 5: OOPS, HERE'S THE BUST

1. "How Do Economists Determine Whether the Economy Is in a Recession?" n.d. The White House. https://www.whitehouse.gov/cea/written-materials/2022/07/21/how-do-economists-determine-whether-the-economy-is-in-a-recession/#:~:text=The%20National%20Bureau%20of%20Economic, committee%20typically%20tracks%20include%20real.
2. "Fiscal Fitness: The U.S. Budget Deficit 's Uncertain Prospects, " *Economic Letter—Insights* 2, no. 4, April 2007, Federal Reserve Bank of Dallas.
3. Joan Robinson, "Reconsideration of the Theory of Free Trade," *Collected Economic Papers,* Volume IV, 1973.
4. Tyler Durden, "The US Consumer Has Cracked: Discover Plunges after 'Shocking' Charge-off Forecast," ZeroHedge, 2023. https://www.zerohedge.com/markets/us-consumer-has-cracked-discover-plunges-after-shocking-charge-forecast?utm_source=&utm_medium=email&utm_campaign=1202.
5. *Business Week*, October 27, 2003.
6. To view recent NIPA data, check the BEA web site at www.bea.doc.gov/bea/dn/nipaweb/SelectTable.asp?Selected=Y.

CHAPTER 6: A MODERN ENIGMA

1. David Walker, Letter, "Report to the Secretary of the Treasury," Financial Audit, Bureau of the Public Debt's Fiscal Years 2007 and 2006 Schedules of Federal Debt, November 2007.
2. Kevin Down, "The Emergence of Fiat Money: A Reconsideration," *Cato Journal,* Winter 2001.
3. Lawrence Parks, "What the President Should Know about Our Monetary System," at www.fame.org, September 12, 1999.
4. Franklin D. Roosevelt, radio address, March 10, 1933.
5. Richard Duncan, *The Dollar Crisis* (Hoboken, NJ: John Wiley & Sons, 2003).
6. Ludwig von Mises, *The Theory of Money and Credit* (Indianapolis, IN: Liberty Fund, 1980).
7. Ibid.
8. Jeffrey M. Herbener, "Ludwig von Mises on the Gold Standard and Free Banking," *Quarterly Journal of Austrian Economics,* Spring 2002.
9. Ibid.

CHAPTER 7: SHORT, UNHAPPY EPISODES IN MONETARY HISTORY

1. "The Trader" column in *Barron's*, March 27, 1933.
2. Ibid., March 13, 1933.
3. Marco Polo and Ronald Latham, *The Travels of Marco Polo,* Penguin, reissued edition, 1958.
4. John Law, quoted in "How John Law's Failed Experiment Gave Us a New Word: Millionaire," at www.freepublic.com.
5. Ibid.
6. Byron King, "Making Money in Early America," *The Daily Reckoning,* December 12, 2004.
7. H. A. Scott Trask, "Inflation and the American Revolution," Mises Organization at www.mises.org, July 18, 2003.
8. John Mackay, in Foreword to Andrew Dickson White, *Fiat Money in France: How It Came, What It Brought, and How It Ended* (Caldwell, ID: Caxton Printers Ltd., 1972; reprint of 1914 original edition).
9. Barry Eichengreen, *Golden Fetters: The Gold Standard and the Great Depression 1919–1939* (New York: Oxford University Press, 1992).
10. Clif Droke, "Paper Money in the Balance," *Gold Digest,* December 13, 2002.
11. Gerald P. Dwyer Jr. and James R. Lothian, "International Money and Common Obstacles in Historical Perspective," at www.independent.org, May 2002.
12. Robert S. Lopez, "The Dollar of the Middle Ages," *Journal of Economic History,* Summer 1951.
13. Nathan Sussman, "Debasements, Royal Revenues, and Inflation in France during the Hundred Years' War," *Journal of Economic History,* March 1993.
14. Peter Spufford, "Le role de la monnaie dans le révolution commerciale du XIII siècle," in *Etudes d'historie monétaire,* Lille, France: Presses universitaires de Lille, 1984.
15. J. M. Cipolla, *Money, Prices, and Civilization in the Mediterranean World, Fifth to Seventeenth Century* (New York: St. Martin's Press, 1967).
16. Dwyer and Lothian, "International Money."
17. Bloomberg.com. 2022. "FTX Bankruptcy Standoff Heats up as Bahamas Challenges US Case," December 14, 2022. https://www.bloomberg.com/news/articles/2022-12-14/ftx-bankruptcy-standoff-heats-up-as-bahamas-challenges-us-case?cmpid=BBD121422_BIZ&utm_medium=email&utm_source=newsletter&utm_term=221214&utm_campaign=bloombergdaily#xj4y7vzkg].
18. Bloomberg.com. 2022. "FTX Kept Your Crypto in a Crypt Not a Vault," November 20, 2022. https://www.bloomberg.com/opinion/articles/2022-11-20/niall-ferguson-ftx-kept-your-crypto-in-a-crypt-not-a-vault.

19. When all is said and done, crypto introduced block chain technology to the world. Block chain promises to bring efficiency to the financial and banking system. It will be as useful as email proved to be following the tech bust in 2000-2001. The dark side of crypto will be block chain based central bank currencies—Central Bank Digital Currencies (CBDC)—making centralized control of the US dollar even more efficient than the digits that move through the internet already.

20. Canadian one dollar coins have loons on them, thus loonies.

21. "U.S. Trade Balance 2021," n.d., Statista. https://www.statista.com/statistics/220041/total-value-of-us-trade-balance-since-2000/#:~:text=As%20 of%202021%2C%20the%20United,about%20763.533%20billion%20 U.S.%20dollars.

22. Warren Buffett, Letter to the Shareholders of Berkshire Hathaway, 2006.

23. Warren Buffett, "America's Growing Trade Deficit Is Selling the Nation Out from under Us," *Fortune,* October 2003.

CHAPTER 8: ALAS, THE DEMISE OF THE DOLLAR

1. Richard Daughty, "A Financial Fiasco," *The Daily Reckoning,* November 24, 2004.

2. Ben Bernanke, "The Chinese Economy: Progress and Challenges," remarks at the Chinese Academy of Social Sciences, Beijing, China, December 15, 2006.

3. Eric J. Fry, "Salvation by Devaluation," *The Daily Reckoning,* January 19, 2004.

4. "Greenspan Sees 'Little' Trouble in Global Current Account Adjustment" press briefing, U.S. Consulate, January 13, 2004, at http://mumbai.usconsulate.gov.

5. Alan Greenspan, remarks at the Bundesbank, Berlin, Germany, January 13, 2004.

6. Adam Smith, *The Wealth of Nations,* 1776.

7. Alan Greenspan, Adam Smith Memorial Lecture, Fife College in Kirkcaldy, Fife, Scotland, February 6, 2005.

8. Alan Greenspan, remarks at the Bundesbank, Berlin, Germany, January 13, 2004.

9. Ibid.

10. Ibid.

11. Ibid.

12. William Meyer, "Warren Buffett's Economic and Political Influence Grows Each Year," *Personal Finance,* May 29, 2004, at www.persfin.co.za.

13. Robert Lenzner and Daniel Kruger, "A Word from a Dollar Bear," *Forbes,* January 10, 2005, at www.forbes.com.

14. Gerald P. Dwyer Jr. and James R. Lothian, "International Money and Common Obstacles in Historical Perspective," at www.independent .org, May 2002.

15. Milton Friedman and Anna J. Schwartz, *A Monetary History of the United States, 1867–1960* (Princeton, NJ: Princeton University Press, 1971).

16. "America Betrayed," Special Report, *Strategic Investment,* 2004.

17. All 2022 growth rates: International Monetary Fund, "Real GDP Growth," Imf.org, 2022, https://www.imf.org/external/datamapper/ NGDP_RPCH@WEO/OEMDC/ADVEC/WEOWORLD.

18. "Production Workers, All Other," Bls.gov, September 9, 2008, https:// www.bls.gov/oes/current/oes519199.htm.

19. U.S. Bureau of Labor Statistics, "Real Earnings Summary," news release no. USDL-23-0018, January 12, 2023, https://www.bls.gov/news.release/realer .nr0.htm#:~:text=From%20December%202021%20to%20December%20 2022%2C%20real%20average%20hourly%20earnings,weekly%20 earnings%20over%20this%20period.

20. Marc Faber, *Tomorrow's Gold* (Hong Kong: CLSA Books, 2003).

21. The mythological power accumulated by Damocles led to him being punished by the tyrant Dionysius I. To teach his rival a lesson, Dionysius I ordered that a sword was to be placed above Damocles' head suspended by a single hair. Because the hair could snap at any time, references to the "sword of Damocles" have come to mean any situation characterized by an ever-present danger.

22. One curious feature of the post-invasion economy is how Russia is trying to circumvent the sanctions imposed on its oil and gas reserves. One example, the Russians sell oil to Indians priced in rubles. The Indians take receipt of the oil, reprice it in dollars, and sell it on the global market. Seems simple enough, but the process adds another middleman and a lot more shipping mileage to each barrel, which also drives the price up.

23. "U.S. National Debt Clock: Real Time," 2019, Usdebtclock.org, https:// www.usdebtclock.org.

24. Fifteen years ago, when we were filming the documentary *I.O.U.S.A.*, we staked out the National Debt Clock in Times Square. There was a running joke at the time that went something like: "If the debt keeps rising, they're going to have to take this one down and add another digit on the sign." It was no joke. Turns out the Debt Clock has been taken down three times since then to add a new digit each time.

25. Sean Corrigan, London correspondent for *The Daily Reckoning,* 2004.

26. Jim Rogers, Essay 12, *The Daily Reckoning,* March 13, 2003.

27. Marc Faber, "The Gloom, Boom, Doom Report," November 2003, at www.gloomboomdoom.com.

28. David Rosenberg, CNN Money, October 3, 2003.

29. Hernando Cortina, Morgan Stanley research note.

30. Asha Bangalore, at www.northerntrust.com, September 19, 2003.

31. "U.S. National Debt Clock: Real Time," 2019, Usdebtclock.org, https://www.usdebtclock.org.
32. James Grant, "The Dollar Meltdown," *Forbes,* October 13, 2003.
33. Stephanie Pomboy, quoted in *The Daily Reckoning,* September 23, 2003.
34. Biography of Ludwig von Mises at www.mises.org.
35. Ludwig von Mises, "Monetary Stabilization and Cyclical Policy," in *On Manipulation of Money and Credit* (Dobbs Ferry, NY: Free Market Books, 1978).
36. Ludwig von Mises, *Human Action: A Treatise on Economics* (Auburn, AL: Ludwig von Mises Institute, 1998).

INDEX

Page numbers followed by *f* refer to figures.

Accenture, 78
Accounting industry, 77–78
Acton, Lord, 24
Adams, John Quincy, 36
Adjustable-rate
    mortgages, 54, 155
The Age of Turbulence
    (Greenspan), 80
Ahmadinejad, Mahmoud, 128
Alameda Research, 126–127
Aldrich, Nelson, 32
Allison, Carolina, 126–127
Amazon, 96
American Eagles, 175
American Express, 72
Andrew, A. Piatt, 32
Argentina, 121
Arthur Andersen, 55, 78, 139

Asian central banks, 152–153
Asian countries, 131
Asian currencies, 75–76
Asset bubbles, 55, 71
Assignats, 120
Augustus, Emperor, 117, 118
Australia, 12, 152, 160

Bahamas, 126
"Bailouts," government, 32
Baker, James, 76
Bangalore, Asha, 166
Bankman-Fried, Sam,
    55, 126–127
Bank of England, 162–163
Bank of Japan, 152, 162
Bank of Korea, 128
Banque de France, 101

Barclays, 80
Barron's, 112
Bastiat, Frédéric, 8–9
BEA (Bureau of Economic
    Analysis), 87, 95
Beijing, China, 135
Berkshire Hathaway, 133, 148
Bernanke, Ben, 54, 55, 57, 59,
    63–65, 67, 78–79, 81, 83, 88,
    132–133, 141, 146, 175
The Big Short (film), 81
Big Tech, 65, 66
Bio tech, 157
Bitcoin, 26, 126, 127
Black Death, 135
Black Wednesday, 163
Block chain, 126
Bloomberg, 81, 91
Bloomsbury Group, 11
Blue-chip stocks, 160
"Blue Magic" (song), 100
Bombay, India, 135
Bond bubble, 73
Bond market, 52, 71, 73, 151
Bonner, Bill, 64
Brady, Tom, 126
Brazil, 148, 166
Bretton Woods Agreement
    and system, 11–15, 17,
    18, 20, 21, 27, 36, 107,
    122–124, 161
British Commonwealth, 12
British empire, 33–34
British pound, 15, 101, 162–163
Bubble economy, 73
Budget deficit(s), 22, 33, 53,
    62–63, 85, 113, 129–130,
    144–146

"Budget surpluses," 40
Buffett, Warren, 133–134,
    148–149, 165
Bündchen, Giesele, 100, 126
Bureau of Economic Analysis
    (BEA), 87, 95
Burns, Arthur, 28
Bush, George H. W., and
    administration, 41
Bush, George W., and
    administration, 40, 41, 85
Business investment, 68,
    94–95, 132
Business Week, 81
"Buy American," 66
Buybacks, 68

Calhoun, John C., 49
California, 36
Calls, 159, 172, 176
Canada, 12, 137
Canadian dollar, 101, 148, 171
Canadian Maple Leafs, 175
Capital inflows, 87–88
Capital investment rate, 72, 93
Capitalism, 28–29, 67, 143
Cargo ships, 103
Caribbean, 137
Carlin, George, 99
Carpeting, 159
"Carry trade," 53
CDs (certificates of deposit),
    172
Center on Budget and Policy
    Priorities, 93
Central America, 66
Central bank(s), 67, 75
    Fed as, 9–10

IMF as, 15
Keynes' vision of
international, 13
Certificates of deposit
(CDs), 172
Chavez, Hugo, 128
"Cheap money," 83–84,
88, 97
Chicago, Ill., 135
China, 27, 29, 43, 61, 66, 71–72,
75, 76, 101, 103, 117–119,
128, 130–132, 135, 137, 141,
152–154, 158–160, 165,
170–171, 174–175, 177.
See also Yuan
Cisco, 169
Citicorp, 69
Citigroup, 80
Civil War, 36, 38, 50, 117, 122
Class warfare, 46
Clinton, Bill, and
administration, 37, 40, 51,
53, 85
Closed-end funds, 156
Clothing, 154, 159
CNBC, 86
CNN, 91
Coal, 178
Coinage, debasement of,
124–125
Cold War, 37
Colombia, 152
Colonialism, 33–34
Columbus, Christopher, 135
Commodities, 101, 123–124,
160, 177–178
Commodity funds, 159
Computer industry, 95, 154

Congress, 45–46, 51
and discussion of public debt,
42–43
economic illiteracy in, 130
power to coin money
granted to, 85
and statutory debt limit, 41
Congressional Budget
Office, 40
Constantine, Emperor, 124
Constitution, 85
Construction, 159
Consumer borrowing, 71, 88
Consumer confidence,
94, 130
Consumer credit (consumer
debt), 56, 64, 89*f,* 116, 138,
139*f,* 141, 155–156, 164
Consumer culture, 60
Consumer price index (CPI),
35, 51–52
Consumer savings, 59–60
Consumer spending, 41, 71,
73, 77, 97
Consumptive debt, 41
Continental money
(continentals), 120
Contracts, enforcement
of, 48
Copper, 178
Corporate bonds, 164
Corporate debt, 164
Corporate profits, 79–80,
93, 96
Corporations, 68
Cortina, Hernando, 165–166
Counterfeiting, 120
Cousins, Norman, 111

COVID-19 pandemic, 4, 22,
48, 55, 63, 64, 68, 76, 96–97,
99, 101, 102, 113, 152,
154, 158–159
CPI (consumer price
index), 35, 51–52
Credit, production vs., 88
Credit bubble, 79
Credit card debt, 66,
155–156, 164
Credit crisis, 73, 138
"Crowding out," 22
Cryptocurrencies, 55,
126–127, 157
Cuba, 112
Cuban Missile Crisis, 17
Currency devaluation, as
policy, 13
Currency fluctuations, 103–104

Daily Reckoning newsletter,
79, 88, 104
Davison, Henry, 32
"Deadweight loss," 47
Debt. *See also* National debt
bailouts and purchasing
of bad, 32
consumer, 56, 64, 66, 116, 138,
139f, 141, 155–156, 164
consumptive, 41
current explosion of, 55–57
definition of, 33
as essential feature of US
economy, 167
good vs. bad, 43–55
government, 33–34, 43,
61–62
institutionalization of, 38–39

mortgage, 59, 164
productive, 41
Debt capitalization, 57
Debt ceiling, 40, 43, 44
Debt limit, statutory, 41
Debt spending, 136
Debt-to-GDP ratio, 45, 45f
Deficits (deficit spending), 33,
39, 44, 45, 47–49, 60–61.
See also Budget deficit(s);
Trade deficits
Deflation, 13, 59, 63, 65, 83
De Gaulle, Charles, 19–20
Demand inflation (demand-pull
inflation), 102, 123
Democrats, 46, 109
Denim jeans, 154
Depressions, 27. *See also* Great
Depression
Derivatives market, 138–139
Dien Bien Phu, battle of, 19
Dillon, Douglas, 20
Dinar, 124
Dollar, United States,
see US dollar
Dollar index (DXY), 101, 102
Dollar Index futures, 171
Dow Theory letters (Russell), 165
Droke, Clif, 124
Ducato, 124
DuPont, 69

Earnings reports, 68
Economic bubbles, 66, 116, 136,
164. *See also specific bubbles*
Economic history, 136
Economic indicators, 72
Economic policy, 51

Economic recovery, 76
Economy, shift in, from
    production to services, 92
Efficient systems, 123
Egypt, ancient, 175
Eichengreen, Barry, 20
Emergency Banking Relief Act
    (1933), 21, 112
Empire of Debt (Wiggin and
    Bonner), 4
Employee stock options, 68
Energy funds, 159
Energy markets, 66
"Enlightened self-interest," 143
Enron, 55, 139
Entrepreneurial culture, 65
Entrepreneurs, 43
ERM (Exchange Rate
    Mechanism), 163, 165
ETFs, *see* Exchange-
    traded funds
Euro, 52, 87, 99, 100, 104,
    124–126, 148, 163, 171, 172
Euro call options, 172
Europe, 16, 142
European Central Bank, 75
European Recovery Plan
    (Marshall Plan), 16
European Union, 86
Exchange-traded funds (ETFs),
    156, 159, 175–176
Executive compensation, 55
Exorbitant Privilege
    (Eichengreen), 20

Faber, Marc, 163
Facebook, 96
Factory jobs, 90–91

Fannie Mae, 79, 138–139, 170
FDI (foreign direct
    investment), 141
Federal Deposit Insurance
    Corporation (FDIC), 112
Federal Open Market
    Committee (FOMC),
    9–10, 78, 80, 84, 150
Federal Reserve (Fed):
  and 2007-2008 financial
    crisis, 54, 83
  as "bubble blower," 73
  as central bank, 9–11
  creation of, 31–32,
    50, 122, 149
  and debt, 57, 59–60, 161, 164
  debt spending as
    policy of, 136
  and deficits, 78
  and of the dollar, 86
  and "full faith and
    credit," 25
  and housing bubble, 74
  and inflation, 51, 52, 75,
    140–142, 144, 152,
    167–168
  interest rates lowered by, 41,
    51, 64, 80, 88–89, 152
  interest rates raised by,
    1, 9, 22, 89
  monetary policies of, 63–65,
    109–110, 113, 114, 132,
    136–137, 141, 149–150,
    155, 177
  money printed by, 21–23, 26,
    106, 111, 173, 174
  and recession, 84–86
  responsibilities of, 150

Federal Reserve (Fed)
(*Continued*)
and solvency of credit
markets, 79
target rate of, 63*f*
and trade deficit,
141–142
and value of the dollar, 127,
149, 163, 174
Federal Reserve Act (1913),
32, 85
Federal Reserve Bank of
Dallas, 85
Federal Reserve Bank of
New York, 16
Federal Reserve Board of
Governors, 150
Ferdinand and Isabella, 119
Ferguson, Niall, 127
Fiat money:
arguments in favor of, 105
and central banks, 127
and declining value of the
dollar, 151
definition of, 25
in history, 118–122
inevitable failure of,
26–27, 104–105, 109,
123, 126, 177
and inflation, 105–106
intrinsic problem
with, 106–107
Keynes and, 29
Mises on, 108
printing of, 51–54, 124
as "smoke and mirrors,"
115–116
Fictitious capitalism, 67, 68

Financial Crisis (2007-2008),
32, 54–55, 78, 80–81, 83,
101, 113, 136, 139, 157
Financial panics, 149–150
Financial Post, 148
Financial Reckoning Day (Wiggin
and Bonner), 4, 66, 68, 127
Financial speculation, 88–90
Floating currencies, 31
Florence, 124
Florin, 124
FOMC, *see* Federal Open
Market Committee
Ford, Gerald, and
administration, 21, 117
Foreclosures, 73, 131
Foreign countries, US dollar
reserves held by, 128–129
Foreign direct investment
(FDI), 141
Foreigners, US debt held by, 43
Foreign investment, 73–74, 77
Forster, E. M., 11
Fort Knox, 25
Founding Fathers, 34
France, 12, 20–21, 27, 87, 100,
101, 117, 119–121, 137
Freddie Mac, 139
Free markets, 24, 29, 107
Free money, 68
French and Indian War, 120
French franc, 20
Friedman, Milton, 150
FTX crypto exchange,
55, 126–127
"Full faith and credit,"
23, 25, 127
Futures, 176–177

G–5 nations, 76
GAO (Government
    Accountability Office), 105
Gas prices, 129, 155
Gates, Bill, 149
GDP, *see* Gross
    domestic product
General Electric, 69
General Motors, 69
Genoa, 124
Genoin, 124
Germany, 13, 16, 27, 112, 117,
    122, 137, 147
Glass-Steagall Act (1933), 112
Global banking system, 103
Globalization, 37, 154, 163
Gold:
    as international margin
        call, 51
    as investment, 115, 117–118,
        160–161, 173–178
    limited world supply of, 23
    as money, 26
    price of, 10, 16, 21–24,
        113–115, 114*f*, 147–148,
        157, 168–169, 174
    rarity of, 123
    restrictions on ownership of,
        21, 107, 112
    and Triffin's paradox,
        100–101
    US reserves of, 14, 17, 20,
        25, 92, 111
Gold coins, 175
Gold exchange-traded
    funds, 175–176
Gold mining stock, 160
Gold options, 176–177

Gold standard:
    arguments against the,
        27–28, 122–123
    and Bretton Woods
        agreement, 14–18, 20, 27
    and currency valuation, 23
    as distant memory, 107
    as economic tool, 26
    and fiat money, 105, 116
    and gold prices, 10–11
    and governments, 109–110
    during Great Depression,
        112, 122–123
    in history, 118, 121–122, 150,
        160–161, 175
    and market for gold, 174
    Nixon's abandonment of, 21,
        24, 27–29, 51, 115, 117–118,
        138, 144, 146, 171, 173, 177
    in postwar period, 21
    and trade gap, 21–22
    and US gold reserves, 14
    and World War I, 25
Government Accountability
    Office (GAO), 105
Governments, as non-producers
    of wealth, 48
Government spending, 44
Grant, Jim, 173
*Grant's Interest Rate
    Observer*, 173
Great Britain (United
    Kingdom), 11–12, 28, 33,
    43, 104, 120, 122–123,
    152, 162–163
Great Depression, 12–13, 21,
    25, 37, 62, 112, 113, 117,
    122, 136, 150

Great Dollar Standard Era, 25, 84, 104, 127–131, 136
"Great Inflation" of the 1970s, 1
Great Society, 28, 34
"Greenback boogie," 10, 63
Green energy, 159
Greenspan, Alan, 41, 54, 55, 57, 60, 61, 65, 67, 75, 78, 80, 85, 88, 141–142, 144–146, 149
Griffin, Edward, 31
Gross, Bill, 75
Gross domestic product (GDP), 40, 45, 45f, 60, 61, 66, 67, 72, 75, 79, 87, 94, 97, 116, 132–133, 137, 145, 162
Group of Ten, 24

Hamilton, Alexander, 34
Harari, Yuval Noah, 11
Hayek, Friedrich, 24
Health care jobs, 64, 116
Hemingway, Ernest, 57
Herbener, Jeffrey M., 109–110
High-tech industries, 95–96
Homebuying, 1
Hong Kong, 137
Hong-Kong Shanghai Banking Company (HSBC), 101
House of Representatives, 44, 46, 47
Housing bubble, 67, 71, 80–81, 91, 131, 133, 136, 139
Housing investment, 73
Housing market, 81, 138–139
Housing permits, 80–81
Housing values, 57

HSBC (Hong-Kong Shanghai Banking Company), 101
Hull, Cordell, 13
Hyperinflation, 132, 147

IBM, 69
IBRD (International Bank for Reconstruction and Development), 14, 16
IMF, see International Monetary Fund
Income tax, 37, 44, 46, 47, 50–51
Index funds, 160, 171
India, 43, 66, 130, 135, 137, 152, 154, 158
Industrial base, 90–91
Industrial production, 90–91
Industrial revolution, 135
Inflation:
    in 1960s and 1970s, 24–25, 28, 51, 157
    from 2013 to 2022, 140f
    in Asia, 152, 153
    and budget deficit, 22
    and cheap money, 97
    current period of, 1–2, 8, 56, 57, 59, 75, 76, 83, 97, 101, 140–146, 167
    demand, 102, 123
    and demise of the dollar, 99, 105–106, 136
    difficulty of containing, 169
    and economic growth, 152–153
    and Fed policy, 63–65, 84–86, 89, 136, 168

and government spending,
44, 48
hidden, 155–156
in history, 35*f,* 117–122, 125
hyper-, 132, 147
and interest rates, 51, 136
in Japan, 60–62
official measures of,
51–52, 75, 94
and oil prices, 129
and opposition to
capitalism, 29
price, 52, 147–149
"real," 53, 94
rising prices as result of, 7
root cause of, 3
and stock market, 167
supply-side, 102–103
and trade deficits, 77, 142
"transitory," 9
Inflation psychosis, 102–103
"Information Age," 67
Information technology (IT),
65
Infrastructure, 14, 56, 93, 118
Institute for Supply
Management (ISM), 54, 72
Interest rates, 63*f*
in 1970s, 41
as arbitrage, 53
effective rates (1955–2020), 9*f*
Fed's lowering of, 41, 51, 64,
80, 88–89, 152
Fed's raising of, 1, 9, 22, 89
in Japan, 62
"overnight Fed funds
rate," 10
and value of the dollar, 150

International Bank for
Reconstruction
and Development
(IBRD), 14, 16
International Monetary Fund
(IMF), 14, 16–18, 166
Investing, 157–169
foreign investments, 160–161
in gold, 175–177
Investment spending, 73
"Invisible hand," 143–144, 146
"iPod economy," 96
Iran, 128
Iraq, 128, 152, 169
Ireland, 137, 152
Iron ore, 178
iShares COMEX Gold
Trust, 176
ISM (Institute for Supply
Management), 54
Israel, 137
Italy, 87, 124

Jackson, Andrew, 36
Jackson, Curtis, 101
Japan, 13, 16, 43, 59, 60–63, 65,
132, 137, 152, 165
Jay-Z, 100
Jefferson, Thomas, 34
Jekyll Island Club, 32
Jobs:
creation of, 93, 130
factory, 90–91
outsourcing of, 153–155
Johnson, Lyndon B., and
administration, 17, 19, 28
Junior gold stocks, 176
Junk bonds, 164

Kelton, Stephanie, 64
Kennedy, John F., 135
Kessler, Andy, 96
Keynes, John Maynard, 11–13, 29, 87, 124
Kiyosaki, Robert, 83
Krugerrands, 175
Kuwait, 128

Labor market, 65, 153–155
Laptop computers, 154
Law, John, 119–120, 127
Legal Tender Act, 117
Lehman Brothers, 55
Lerner, Abba, 42
"Leveraging" assets, 65
Lincoln, Abraham, 117, 122
Lobbying, 47
London Gold Pool, 17
Long Beach, Calif., 103
Los Angeles, Calif., 135
Louisiana territory, 34, 120
Louis XIV, King, 119
Luxembourg, 43, 137

McGovern, George, 53
Mackay, John, 120–121
MacroMavens, 171
Madison, James, 36
"Making Less Than Dad" (CNN headline), 91
Manufacturing, 54, 64, 66, 96, 116, 138, 159, 163, 168–169
Margin calls, 19
Marshall, George, 16
Marshall Plan, 16
"Maximum point of revenue" (taxation), 49
Medicaid, 38

Medicare, 38–40, 105, 164
Mercantilism, 71
Mergers and acquisitions, 68
Merrill Lynch, 80, 164
Meta, 96
Mexican War, 36
Mexico, 12, 117, 119, 137
Microchips, 66
Military spending, 37
Mises, Ludwig von, 24, 108, 173–174
Mississippi Scheme, 127
Modern monetary theory (MMT), 22, 64
Monetary policy, 50, 51, 109
Money, 111–112. *See also* Fiat money
  power to coin, 85
  printing, 21–23, 26, 51–54, 106, 111, 118, 124, 173, 174, 177
  as store of value, 127
  and tangible value, 26
Morgan, J. P., 31
Morgan Stanley, 80, 162, 166
Morris, Robert, 120
Mortgage-backed securities, 138–139
Mortgage Bankers Association, 54
Mortgage bubble, 41
Mortgage debt, 59, 164
Mortgage payments, 54
Mortgage refinancing bubble, 73, 91
Motorola, 56
Mutual funds, 61, 156, 159, 160, 176

Nasdaq, 147
National Association
 of REALTORS
 (NAR), 131, 139
National Bureau of Economic
 Research (NBER), 84
National debt, 36–43, 38*f*
 ballooning of, 105, 161, 164
 and budget deficits, 22
 complacency about, 39
 deficit spending vs., 33
 and Fed policy, 44, 67, 74,
  75, 146, 152
 held by foreign central banks,
  43, 153, 160
 in history, 36–38, 50, 51, 117
 and inflation, 149
 interest on, 170
 as share of GDP, 45, 61,
  116
 and trade deficits, 52–53, 143
 unsustainability of, 144–145
National Economists Club, 59
National Income and Product
 Accounts (NIPA), 96
National parks, 42
Nazis, 122
NBER (National Bureau of
 Economic Research), 84
Nero, 117, 118
Nestlé, 72
Netflix, 96
Netherlands, 137
New Deal, 37
Newmont Mining, 176
New Orleans Investment
 Conference, 165
New York City, 100, 135

*New York Times Annual Financial
 Review,* 149
New Zealand, 12
9/11, 37, 41, 113
NIPA (National Income and
 Product Accounts), 96
Nixon, Richard, and
 administration, 18, 21,
 23–28, 51–53, 115, 117, 118,
 122, 137–138, 161, 171, 177
"Nixon Shock," 28
Northern Trust, 166
Nussle, Jim, 37–38

Office of Management and
 Budget, 37–38
Oil (oil prices), 23–24, 101, 129,
 157–159, 158*f,* 178
O'Neill, Paul, 40
Open-end funds, 156
Optimism, false sense of, 75
Options, 157, 159, 160, 176–177
Organization for Economic
 Cooperation and
 Development (OECD), 61
Organization of Petroleum
 Exporting Countries
 (OPEC), 128, 159
Outsourcing, 153–155
"Overnight Fed funds rate," 10
Owen-Glass Act, 50

Panic of 1893, 31
Panic of 1907, 31, 149
Paper money, 26, 117–124, 127
"Parable of the Broken
 Window" (Bastiat), 8–9
"Paradigm of flexibility," 146

Paulson, Henry "Hank,"
    32, 37–38, 83
Payment currency, 99, 101–103
Pension obligations, 70
Pension plan assets, 69
People's Republic of
    Congo, 152
Peron, Juan, 121
Personal consumption, 72, 132
Personal savings rate, 72, 88, 89*f*
Peter G. Peterson
    Foundation, 105
Petrochemicals, 159
Pierce, Franklin, 36
Pinker, Steven, 11
Polo, Marco, 119
Pomboy, Stephanie, 171
Powell, Jerome "Jay," 9–10, 57,
    64, 83, 88, 89, 141, 149, 156
Price inflation, 52, 147–149
Production, credit vs., 88
Productive debt, 41, 43
Productivity, 64, 75, 86,
    92–93, 95, 128
Profit motive, 65
Profits, corporate, 79–80, 93, 96
Protectionism, 144
Purchasing power, 75–76
Putin, Vladimir, 128
Puts, 176

Quantitative easing (QE), 64, 83

Ratings agencies, 54
Reagan, Ronald, and
    administration, 37, 41–42, 63
Real, Brazilian, 148

"Real economy," 71, 96
Real estate speculation, 135
Real productivity, 64
Recessions, 78, 84, 90
Republicans, 46, 109
Reserve currency, 101
Restructuring, 61–62
Retail jobs, 64, 116
Retirement saving, 105–106
Reuters, 80
Revolutionary War (War for
    Independence), 34, 50, 120
"Revolving door," 47
Rickards, Jim, 99
Roach, Stephen, 73, 162
Robinson, Joan, 87
Rogers, Jim, 68, 149, 162
Roman Empire, 27, 117, 118, 124
Roosevelt, Franklin Delano,
    and administration, 37, 51,
    106–107, 112, 117, 122
Rosenberg, David, 164
Rubin, Robert, 40
"Rubinomics," 40, 53
Ruble, 112, 128, 158
Russell, Richard, 165
Russia, 67, 112, 128, 137, 158.
    See also Ukraine, Russian
    invasion of

Safety trades, 101
San Francisco, Calif., 81
Sarbanes-Oxley Act (2002), 77
Saudi Arabia, 100, 101, 128, 152
Savings (savings rates), 59–60,
    71, 79, 131, 151, 166
Savings glut, 133

Schiff, Jacob, 149
Schwartz, Anna J., 150
SDRs (Special Drawing
    Rights), 17–18
Securities and Exchange
    Commission (SEC), 78
Senate, 46, 47
Senior gold stocks, 176
Service sector, 54, 64,
    92, 116, 130
Seventh Amendment, 50
Shanghai, China, 135
Shays, Daniel, 121
Shays' Rebellion, 121
Shelton, Arthur, 32
Singapore, 137
Smith, Adam, 44, 143–144
Snow, John, 161, 168
Social Security, 38–40, 105, 164
Solidus, 124
Soros, George, 149,
    163, 165, 169
Sound money, 8, 15, 85
South African Krugerrands, 175
South Korea, 128, 137, 152
Sovereign wealth funds
    (SWFs), 132
Soviet Union, 12, 147, 154
S&P (Standard & Poor's), 69
S&P 500 companies, 97
Spaghetti Westerns, 2
Spain, 27, 117, 119
Spanish Inquisition, 119
Special Drawing Rights
    (SDRs), 17–18
Speculation, 120
Stagflation, 165
Standard of living, 2

Standard & Poor's (S&P), 69
Stimulus checks, 48, 64, 103
Stockholders, 56–57, 78
Stock market, 70, 71, 73, 131,
    133, 151, 160, 167–168
Stock market crash (1929), 62,
    113
Stock options, employee, 68
Stock prices, 70
Stock values, 57
Stumpf, John, 81
Subprime adjustable-rate
    mortgages, 54, 73, 131
Subprime mortgage crisis, 136
Subprime mortgages, 80
Substitution effect, 94
Sudan, 129
Supply and demand, 20–21, 26,
    115, 116, 123, 175
Supply chains, 103
Supply-side inflation, 102–103
Supreme Court, 37, 44
Sweden, 137
Swedish krona, 101, 171
SWFs (sovereign wealth
    funds), 132
Swiss franc, 101, 171
Switzerland, 137

Taiwan, 66, 137
Tangible assets, 178
Tangible capital investment, 70
Tangible capital stock, 70
Tariffs, 49, 51, 138
Tax cuts, 46, 59
Tax policy, 47, 49–50
Tax rebates, 72
Tax revenues, 44

Tech bubble (early 2000s),
55, 101
Templeton, Sir John,
149, 164–165
Terrorism, 129, 159, 169
"Thanksgiving dinner" (metric),
2
Tight money, 84–86
TikTok, 96
Time magazine, 20
Torquenada, Tomás de, 119
Trade barriers, 13
Trade deficits, 21–22, 52–53,
63, 74–77, 107–108, 117,
129–130, 140, 142–143,
148, 160, 162, 173
Trade gap, 77, 132, 142
Trade surplus, 16, 107, 131
Transitory inflation, 9
Treasury securities, 53, 137,
150, 152, 164
"Trickle-down" revenues, 48
Triffin, Robert, 100–102
Triffin's paradox, 100–104, 131
Truman, Harry S., 14
Trump, Donald, 43, 47
Tungsten, 178
Turkey, 137, 166
Tyco, 55

UBS, 101
Ukraine, Russian invasion of,
23, 29, 66, 103, 158
Unemployment, 13, 24,
25, 78, 167
United Airlines, 69
United Kingdom, *see*
Great Britain

United States:
and Bretton Woods
Agreement, 11–14
economic weakness of,
74–75
in eighteenth century, 120
exports from, 92
gold reserves of, 17, 20
inflation, from 2013 to
2022, 140*f*
"net worth" of, 42
in nineteenth century, 122
territorial expansion of,
36–37
USA Today, 146
US Commerce Department, 80,
81, 93, 95
US dollar:
as America's most successful
export, 163
and Asian currencies,
152, 160
and Bretton Woods
system, 24, 27
buying power of,
over time, 35*f*
and Canadian dollar, 100
in circulation, 114*f*
currencies pegged to,
14, 27
declining value of the,
8, 22, 23, 29, 34–36, 53,
73, 86–87, 91, 94, 106,
133, 136–137, 141–142,
149–151
demise of the, 2, 19–20,
27, 34, 60, 90, 112–115,
127–131, 169–178

and euro, 52, 104
and fiscal deficits, 47
foreign holdings of,
73–77, 152–153
global economy and
weakening, 137
and gold standard,
10–11, 14, 15–18
in Great Dollar Standard Era,
25, 84, 104, 127–131, 136
hedging against the, 160–169
and inflation, 35*f*, 147–149,
155–156
and interest rates, 10
as international reserve
currency, 3, 15, 64, 99,
103, 122, 135
as IOU, 23, 111
and Japanese yen, 60–62
and national debt, 33, 67, 143
and oil, 158
patriotic faith in the, 70–71
as payment currency, 103
possible events leading to
sudden drop in value
of, 128–131
and trade deficit, 140
and Triffin's paradox,
100–103
US Dollar Index
(USDX), 171–172
"US International Investment
Position" (BEA report), 87
US Treasury Department, 26,
32, 34, 37–38, 40, 60, 64, 74,
76, 100, 161

Vanderlip, Frank, 32

Venezuela, 128
Venice, 124
Veterans' health care, 105
Vietnam, 19, 154
Volcker, Paul, 63
"Voodoo economics," 41

Wage and price controls,
24–25, 51, 115, 138
Wages and salaries, 64, 93,
116, 153–155
Walker, David, 105
Wall Street, 47, 68, 84, 113
Walpole, Robert, 33
Warburg, Paul, 32, 149
Warburton, Peter, 52
War for Independence, *see*
Revolutionary War
War of 1812, 36, 50
War on Poverty, 19
War on Terror, 37, 41, 113
Wars and military campaigns,
50, 57, 170
Wealth, 86, 90
Wealth creation, 57, 71
Wealth-driven spending, 85
Weimar Republic, 122, 147
Wells Fargo, 81
White, Harry Dexter, 11–14
White House Council of
Economic Advisers, 132
Wiggin Sessions (podcast), 4, 26
Wilson, Woodrow, and
administration, 32, 51
Wolfe, Virginia, 11
Working capital ratio, 56
World Bank, 14, 15
World banking system, 108

World Trade Organization,
    141
World War I, 25, 37
World War II, 11, 13, 122

XAU Index, 169

Yastrzemski, Carl, 7
Yellen, Janet, 55, 57, 65, 88, 141
Yen, Japanese, 99, 162
"Yen miracle," 60
Yuan, Chinese, 99, 101,
    124, 158, 160